Reading Habits in the COVID-19 Pandemic

Abigail Boucher • Marcello Giovanelli
Chloe Harrison • Robbie Love
Caroline Godfrey

Reading Habits in the COVID-19 Pandemic

An Applied Linguistic Perspective

Abigail Boucher
School of Social Sciences
and Humanities
Aston University
Birmingham, UK

Marcello Giovanelli
School of Social Sciences
and Humanities
Aston University
Birmingham, UK

Chloe Harrison
School of Social Sciences
and Humanities
Aston University
Birmingham, UK

Robbie Love
School of Social Sciences
and Humanities
Aston University
Birmingham, UK

Caroline Godfrey
School of Social Sciences
and Humanities
Aston University
Birmingham, UK

ISBN 978-3-031-52752-4   ISBN 978-3-031-52753-1 (eBook)
https://doi.org/10.1007/978-3-031-52753-1

© The Editor(s) (if applicable) and The Author(s), under exclusive licence to Springer Nature Switzerland AG 2024

This work is subject to copyright. All rights are solely and exclusively licensed by the Publisher, whether the whole or part of the material is concerned, specifically the rights of translation, reprinting, reuse of illustrations, recitation, broadcasting, reproduction on microfilms or in any other physical way, and transmission or information storage and retrieval, electronic adaptation, computer software, or by similar or dissimilar methodology now known or hereafter developed.

The use of general descriptive names, registered names, trademarks, service marks, etc. in this publication does not imply, even in the absence of a specific statement, that such names are exempt from the relevant protective laws and regulations and therefore free for general use.

The publisher, the authors, and the editors are safe to assume that the advice and information in this book are believed to be true and accurate at the date of publication. Neither the publisher nor the authors or the editors give a warranty, expressed or implied, with respect to the material contained herein or for any errors or omissions that may have been made. The publisher remains neutral with regard to jurisdictional claims in published maps and institutional affiliations.

Cover pattern © Melisa Hasan

This Palgrave Macmillan imprint is published by the registered company Springer Nature Switzerland AG.
The registered company address is: Gewerbestrasse 11, 6330 Cham, Switzerland

Paper in this product is recyclable.

ACKNOWLEDGEMENTS

We are grateful to all those who responded to our survey, without whom this book would not have been possible. We would also like to thank both the Department of English, Languages and Applied Linguistics at Aston University and the Aston Centre for Applied Linguistics for supporting our research.

Contents

1 Introduction — 1

2 Reading, Genre, and Crisis — 13

3 Reading and Time — 39

4 Reading as a Coping Strategy — 63

5 Re-reading in the Pandemic — 83

6 Lockdown Experiences of Social Reading — 105

7 Conclusion — 125

Appendix 1 *The Lockdown Library Project*: Survey Questions — 131

Appendix 2 Top 10 Open Questions by Total Response Token Count — 139

Appendix 3 Top 100 Keywords in the Free-Text Portion of the *Aston Lockdown Reading Survey* Corpus — 141

Index — 145

List of Tables

Table 1.1	Metadata attributes of the *Aston Lockdown Reading Survey Corpus*	5
Table 1.2	Distribution of question responses and tokens by participant gender identity	5
Table 1.3	Distribution of question responses and tokens by participant age group	6
Table 1.4	Distribution of question responses and tokens by question type	6
Table 2.1	Summary of responses to Question 11.i	24
Table 2.2	Summary of responses to Question 15	24
Table 2.3	Summary of responses to Question 11.iii	25
Table 2.4	Summary of responses to Question 21	25
Table 2.5	Summary of responses to Question 11.ii	26
Table 2.6	Summary of responses to Question 16	27
Table 2.7	Summary of responses to Question 11.iv	30
Table 2.8	Summary of responses to Question 22	31
Table 3.1	Summary of responses to Question 5	44
Table 3.2	Frequency rank of the ten most frequently occurring noun lemmas in the Question 5a sub-corpus	52
Table 3.3	Top modifiers of 'time' in the Question 5a sub-corpus	53
Table 3.4	Top verb collocates with 'time' as their object	54
Table 3.5	Sample concordance lines for *reading*	56
Table 4.1	Top 100 keywords thematically grouped	69
Table 4.2	Top 20 collocates of *comfort* in the open question sub-corpus	71
Table 4.3	Top 10 collocates of *comforting* in the open question sub-corpus	71

Table 4.4	Wordforms of ESCAPE in the open question sub-corpus	75
Table 4.5	Wordforms of DISTRACT in the open question sub-corpus	77
Table 5.1	Summary of responses to Question 24	88
Table 5.2	Summary of responses to Question 24a	88
Table 5.3	Which books do you re-read? Summary of top participant responses for before and since lockdown	89

CHAPTER 1

Introduction

Abstract In this chapter we introduce the book and the project, outlining the background to the study, our research methodology and design, and an overview of the headlines of the data. We explain our mixed-methods approach, which combines quantitative analyses of discrete survey data with corpus-based and qualitative analyses of participants' free-text responses. We also briefly summarise the main chapters, outlining how each makes a contribution to our study and to our overall understanding of reading habits during the pandemic.

Keywords Methodology • Qualitative analysis • Quantitative analysis • Reading habits

1 COVID-19, Lockdown and Reading

On 16 March 2020, the then Prime Minister of the United Kingdom, Boris Johnson, announced that, in the midst of rising cases of Coronavirus disease 2019 (COVID-19), 'now is the time for everyone to stop non-essential contact and travel' (Gov UK 2020a). A week later, the first lockdown period was announced, coming legally into effect 3 days later on 26 March. At this point, stay at home measures came into force which meant that schools and universities were closed and the public were only allowed

© The Author(s), under exclusive license to Springer Nature Switzerland AG 2024
A. Boucher et al., *Reading Habits in the COVID-19 Pandemic*,
https://doi.org/10.1007/978-3-031-52753-1_1

to go out for household shopping and limited exercise (one form per day), to seek medical help or to provide care for a vulnerable person, or to travel to work if a *keyworker* defined as those, for example, working in health and social care, education, and public services (Gov UK 2020b). Between May and August 2020, these restrictions were eased and other measures brought in, such as the 2 m social distancing rule and guidance on group gatherings. Additional regional and national lockdowns and restrictions followed throughout the period leading to the end of December 2021.[1]

In a general sense, we know that the public's relationship with books changed during the lockdown months. Studies and reports have highlighted the increased number of books sold during the pandemic (BBC 2020; Flood 2020a) and how, in particular, both longform novels (Flood 2020b) and poetry (Bravo 2020) were bringing the nation together with a shared purpose of reading to cope. In fact, the relationship between a reader's engagement with novels and their subsequent ordering of temporal experience is a key theme that emerges from Davies et al.'s (2022) study of novel reading during the pandemic. They demonstrate how reading gave many people living through lockdown a way of 'reckoning with pandemic time' by providing 'a specific structuring purpose' (2022, p. 27). In a broader social context, The Reading Agency (2020) even claimed that their 'New survey says reading connects a nation in lockdown' and community reading projects also took off as readers found ways of discussing books in online spaces. Northington (2021), for example, suggests that the pandemic resulted in 'fellow book lovers [...] banding together, supporting each other and reaching out to those in need', implying that readers offered each other a form of community support and even, perhaps, an informal counselling service. We also know, however, that some readers, often the most vulnerable and/or with limited access to new ways of accessing and talking about books, were deeply affected by the restrictions. For example, in their study of the impact of lockdowns on UK libraries, McMenemy et al. (2023) highlight how the closure and subsequent restricted services offered by libraries meant that tens of millions of books were not borrowed compared to pre-lockdown years.

In this book, we specifically focus on the impact of the first lockdown period (March–July 2020) on UK public reading habits. We explore the extent to which the consequences of lockdown measures, such as working from home, home-schooling, the loss of opportunities to engage in leisure

---

[1] A useful timeline outlining government measures between March 2020 and December 2021 can be found at Institute for Government (2022).

pursuits that involved leaving the home and/or mixing with others, as well as general anxieties about the pandemic and what the future might hold, affected readers' relationships with books and reading. Our book thus provides, to our knowledge, the first study that draws on a set of applied linguistic methodologies and a broad range of linguistic methods to examine how public reading habits changed in those first weeks of what was a remarkable moment in our history. Our book makes key contributions to applied linguistics, health humanities, stylistics, and the sociolinguistics of reading, enhancing our understanding of the ways in which the first lockdown impacted on reading and revealing important and novel insights with regards to the relationship between readers and reading practices during that time.

2 The *Aston Lockdown Reading Survey Corpus*

The contents of this book are drawn from data that form the *Aston Lockdown Reading Survey Corpus*,[2] which in turn arose from *The Lockdown Library Project*,[3] a study of UK reading during the first lockdown, that we ran from 1 July–31 August 2020. The project survey addressed the following research questions:

> RQ1: How has the pandemic affected the quantity of books people are reading?
> RQ2: How has the pandemic influenced the type/genre of books people are reading?
> RQ3: How has the pandemic influenced people to return to previously read books?
> RQ4: How has the pandemic made people access and talk about books in new/different ways?

We hosted the survey on and administered it through www.onlinesurveys.ac.uk, distributing it via multiple social media channels, our own

---

[2] The full *Aston Lockdown Reading Survey Corpus* is available publicly via Aston University's institutional research data repository, *Aston Data Explorer* (URL: https://doi.org/10.17036/researchdata.aston.ac.uk.00000602).

[3] See the project website for more details https://lockdownlibraryproject.wordpress.com/. The survey questions can be found in Appendix 1. Given that our data are drawn from UK respondents during a specific time period, we are aware that we cannot make wider claims about reading habits in other countries or at other moments during the pandemic. We hope, however, that our methods, results, and analyses will be of interest to researchers working in other contexts.

institution's website, and *Call for Participants* (https://www.callforparticipants.com), a platform that advertises academic research to the general public. In total 860 participants living in the UK completed the survey; we outline more details about our corpus in Sect. 3.

3 METHODOLOGY

3.1 Applied Linguistics

In this book, we draw on a number of methodologies and methods within the broad discipline of applied linguistics, defined by Schmitt and Cele-Murcia (2020, p. 1) as 'using what we know about (a) language, (b) how it is learned and (c) how it is used, in order to achieve some purpose or solve some problem in the real world'. In the case of our book, we draw on theoretical knowledge and ways of generating, presenting, and analysing empirical data from linguistics and apply these in order to understand reading habits in the lockdown by examining the language that our participants use to talk about them. In other words, our investigation is an essentially *linguistic* one that aims to understand an important moment in our lived experience (the *application*). Specifically, as academics we work within the areas of genre studies (Boucher), the sociology of reading (Godfrey), literary linguistics (Giovanelli and Harrison), and corpus linguistics (Love). Consequently principles, approaches, and methods from these fields (and others when needed) also inform the ways that we work with and analyse our data. We have, as appropriate, outlined and explained these in more detail in each respective chapter, mindful of the fact that all analytical approaches are necessarily driven by the researcher's professional judgement in choosing 'the right tool for the right job' (Saldaña 2011, pp. 177–178). In Sect. 3.2, however, we discuss our corpus and provide a short overview of the general approach we took.

3.2 Analysis of the Corpus

The *Aston Lockdown Reading Survey Corpus* comprises all of the responses to our survey questions, totalling 200,245 tokens. Using 'modest' Extensible Markup Language (XML) (Hardie 2014), the corpus is marked up to capture the metadata attributes as highlighted in Table 1.1.

The distribution of survey responses according to the gender identity and age range of participants is presented in Tables 1.2 and 1.3.

1 INTRODUCTION   5

Table 1.1 Metadata attributes of the *Aston Lockdown Reading Survey Corpus*

XML attribute	Description	Example
URN	Unique response number (URN), automatically assigned by the survey software	'606,218-606,209-62,332,731'
Respondent_id	Unique participant ID code corresponding to the URN, used in the reporting of individual responses	'1'
Age_range	Participant age category	'31-40'
Occupation	Participant occupation (uncategorised free text)	'English teacher'
Gender	Participant gender identity (categorised free text)	'Female'
q_id	Survey question number	'5'
q_type	Survey question type (open or closed)	'Closed'
q_prompt	Survey question prompt text	'5. Since the start of the lockdown, I have been reading'

Table 1.2 Distribution of question responses and tokens by participant gender identity[a]

Gender	Participant count	Question response count	Token count
Female	686	25,191	162,769
Male	138	4704	29,178
Prefer not to say/blank	13	781	2707
Non-binary	7	295	4227
Agender	1	50	365
Genderqueer	2	79	440
Genderfluid	1	34	323
Gender neutral	1	44	236
Total	*849*	*31,178*	*200,245*

[a] Given the need to obtain survey data fairly quickly to capture reflections on the first lockdown period, we used convenience sampling in that our respondents self-selected to take part and we played no mediating role in that selection. We are aware that 80.8% of our survey respondents reported their gender as 'female' and that there is subsequently an imbalance and overrepresentation of females, which makes generalisability impossible. However, qualitative analysis of our data still provides, we believe, rich and valid evidence of the ways in which individuals perceived changes in their reading habits during the lockdown; see also Chap. 7 for discussion

Table 1.3 Distribution of question responses and tokens by participant age group

Age	Question response count	Token count
18-30	6848	47,213
31-40	7618	49,665
41-50	6974	43,797
51-60	6057	36,431
61-70	2691	16,632
70+	877	5741
Blank	113	766
Total	*31,178*	*200,245*

Table 1.4 Distribution of question responses and tokens by question type

Question type	Question response count	Token count
Closed	24,248	113,546
Open	6930	86,699
Total	*31,178*	*200,245*

We analysed the survey data using a range of quantitative and qualitative approaches. Whereas responses to the closed questions were analysed quantitatively, responses to the open questions were qualitatively examined, drawing on a sub-corpus of free-text responses to the open questions, containing 6930 individual responses and running to 86,699 tokens (see Table 1.4). In these cases, and drawing on established methods of qualitatively analysing data, we employed thematic coding (e.g. Auerbach and Silverstein 2003; Saldaña 2021; Braun and Clarke 2022) in order to identify emerging patterns in responses and group them together to create an analytical narrative. As Gibbs (2018, p. 38) outlines, 'Coding is a way of indexing or categorizing the text in order to establish a framework of thematic ideas about it'. In the chapters in this book, these themes provide the structure for our analytical sections. This kind of qualitative approach works particularly well when examining the rich variation in description and motivation inherent in datasets generated from human accounts of experience (see Tracy 2020, pp. 6–7).

In addition, some strands of our analysis of open question responses were complemented by the use of methods from corpus linguistics, which, in general, involves applying computational techniques to (usually large)

samples of language data 'to obtain information about frequencies, co-occurrences and meanings' (Hunston 2022, p. 1). Language samples that are examined in this way are known as *corpora* (singular: *corpus*); a corpus is 'some set of machine-readable texts which is deemed an appropriate basis on which to study a specific set of research questions' (McEnery and Hardie 2012, p. 1).

The value of such methods for exploring patterns in the discursive construction of meaning across multiple textual samples is demonstrated by research in corpus-assisted discourse studies (CADS; Partington et al. 2013). CADS combines principles from corpus linguistics and discourse analysis to effectively increase the scale of observations compared to manual qualitative analysis alone (see e.g. Gillings et al. 2023; Taylor and Marchi 2018). Furthermore, corpus methods have been shown to provide insight as a complementary approach specifically for the exploration of free-text survey data (e.g. Huntley et al. 2018; Brookes and Baker 2022; McClaughlin et al. 2023), as summarised by McGlaughlin et al. (2023, p. 14), who found that:

> corpus analysis of the open-ended survey questions surfaced a more nuanced patterning in responses, and at a faster pace of analysis, than would be possible through manual thematic analysis of survey responses

Where corpus methods were used, we analysed the data using *Sketch Engine* (Kilgarrif et al. 2004, 2014), a commercial corpus query system which can process XML mark-up to facilitate the creation and analysis of user-specified sub-corpora, in this instance the sub-corpus of responses to open questions. All spelling, phrasing, and syntax in the data were maintained and are reproduced as they were originally written by participants.

4 Structure of the Book

This book is structured so as to provide a uniform approach to each chapter, with a short introduction, an overview of context and a relevant literature review, a note on methodology, an analysis of specific parts of the survey corpus data, and then a conclusion.

Following this chapter, Chap. 2 ('Reading, Genre, and Crisis') surveys the literature on the relationship between pandemics, literature (especially the role played by genre and popular fiction) and reading habits. Drawing on previous studies, we first examine how world pandemics and public health emergencies involving widespread illness have had significant literary and cultural impacts. We specifically examine the relationship of particular genres to times of crisis highlighting how, historically, crisis is manifested often through the production and consumption of genre fiction (as opposed to what might be considered 'literary' fiction) and how there is a long history of readers both confronting and escaping anxieties and escaping through genre fiction. We explore how genre fiction may be a prism through which we can understand contemporary events and provide readers with the distance to work through contemporary anxieties. We then turn to our data by examining the genres that participants in our survey said they read more and those which they said they avoided—and their reasons for doing so. Our analysis demonstrates the relationship between particular genres of literature and the need to cope at a time of crisis.

Chapter 3 ('Reading and Time') examines how participants reported that the lockdown period had affected the amount that they read. We begin by providing an overview of the likely effect of lockdown on participants' time, for example, in the reduction of commuting and the increase in home working and home-schooling children, both of which may have impacted on time that was previously used for reading or may have, conversely, provided opportunities for reading that did not previously exist. We then turn to our data to focus on two key findings. First, we examine how participants reported the effect of gaining or losing time on the amount they read (more or less than pre-pandemic). Specifically we draw on a small sub-corpus of free-text responses to a single survey question about the amount of time participants spent reading during the lockdown. Here, participants' use of the word *time* is explored via the computational analysis of its collocations, 'combinations of words that habitually co-occur in texts' (Brezina 2018, p. 67). Second, we look at how our participants perceived their use of time and their use of particular metaphors to frame their understanding of time related to the quality and quantity of their reading. Within this second focus, we draw on a sample of concordance lines (words in the context in which they appear in the corpus) to examine how reading itself is often personified and presented as an agentive figure acting on the reader through time.

Chapter 4 ('Reading as a Coping Strategy') focuses specifically on reading as a coping strategy. We first draw on the relationship between reading and wellbeing and examine some of the ways that reading has been known to have therapeutic value. We then examine how participants reported their use of reading as a positive coping strategy, analysing the reasons they provided for why they turned to reading, and drawing attention to the ways in which they framed their experiences. The final part of this chapter discusses findings more broadly to suggest how our data builds on and extends what we know about how reading might be used for wellbeing purposes during times of crisis. Chapter 4 thus takes a broader perspective of the data by analysing the full sub-corpus of free-text responses to all open questions. Here, we employed keyness analysis to automatically extract terms (known as *keywords* or *key items*; see Gabrielatos 2018) that are relatively frequent across the open question responses compared to a reference corpus, thus identifying 'signposts' to potentially interesting themes by highlighting lexically salient concepts and ideas (Baker 2018).

Chapter 5 ('Re-reading in the Pandemic') develops the discussion in Chaps. 3 and 4 by examining how participants in our data reported returning to books that they had previously read which offered familiarity, reliability, nostalgia and thus provided a coping mechanism. The chapter begins with a survey of the latest research in re-reading as a phenomenon, drawing on theoretical and empirical studies that have sought to explore why people re-read and the personal benefits of re-reading fiction. We then turn to our data to explore the reasons participants gave us for returning to particular books or reading habits from before the pandemic, and we examine the ways in which they talked about the emotional, immersive, and parasocial aspects of re-reading. We then look at the specific ways that they explain their reasons for re-reading books. In this latter respect, we examine the metaphors, generally concerned with reassurance and the emotional support brought about by returning to familiar storylines, that readers draw on to frame their re-reading choices and to reveal their motivations for re-reading.

Chapter 6 ('Lockdown Experiences of Social Reading') examines a number of related issues and findings concerned with the social aspect of reading and how the pandemic may have altered the ways that participants accessed books and discussed their reading with others. We first explore both the personal and social practices of reading, examining what we know about reading in social contexts. We examine how COVID-19 undoubtedly affected the ways in which these practices are conceived and undertaken by readers, highlighting the increased affordances of online tools such as Zoom and MS Teams to set up virtual reading groups. We then turn to our data to consider two specific questions, comparing reported behaviours pre-pandemic and during the pandemic: participants' preferred way of reading, and how frequently and in what formats they talked about their reading with others. The chapter thus explores the extent to which participants perceived the pandemic had affected the specific formats and situations in which books were read and or discussed.

Finally, Chap. 7 provides a summary of our key findings and some final reflections on the project and the book.

References

Auerbach, Carl, and Louise B. Silverstein. 2003. *Qualitative data: An introduction to coding and analysis*. New York: New York University Press.

Baker, Paul. 2018. Keywords: Signposts to objectivity? In *The corpus linguistics discourse: In honour of Wolfgang Teubert*, ed. Anna Čermáková and Michaela Mahlklberg, 77–94. Amsterdam: John Benjamins.

BBC. 2020. Coronavirus: book sales surge as readers seek escapism and education. *BBC News*. https://www.bbc.co.uk/news/entertainment-arts-52048582. Accessed 16 June 2023.

Braun, Virginia, and Victoria Clarke. 2022. *Thematic analysis: A practical guide*. London: Sage.

Bravo, Lauren. 2020. How poetry came to save us in lockdown. Penguin. https://www.penguin.co.uk/articles/2020/05/lockdown-poetry-phenomenon-pharmacy. Accessed 27 August 2023.

Brezina, Vaclav. 2018. *Statistics in corpus linguistics: A practical guide*. Cambridge: Cambridge University Press.

Brookes, Gavin, and Paul Baker. 2022. Cancer services patient experience in England: Quantitative and qualitative analyses of the National Cancer Patient Experience Survey. *BMJ Supportive and Palliative Care*. https://doi.org/10.1136/spcare-2022-003543.

Davies, Ben, Christina Lupton, and Johanne Gormsen Schmidt. 2022. *Reading novels during the Covid-19 pandemic*. Oxford: Oxford University Press.

Flood, Alison. 2020a. Britons are reading more in lockdown, says survey for World Book Night. *The Guardian*, April 23.

———. 2020b. Have you been using the pandemic to catch up on long classic novels? *The Guardian*, October 27.

Gabrielatos, Costas. 2018. Keyness analysis: Nature, metrics and techniques. In *Corpus approaches to discourse: A critical review*, ed. Charlotte Taylor and Anna Marchi, 225–258. London: Routledge.

Gibbs, Graham R. 2018. *Analysing qualitative data*. 2nd ed. London: Sage.

Gillings, Mathew, Gerlinde Mautner, and Paul Baker. 2023. *Corpus-assisted discourse studies*. Cambridge: Cambridge University Press.

Gov UK. 2020a. Prime Minister's statement on coronavirus (COVID-19): 23 March 2020. https://www.gov.uk/government/speeches/pm-address-to-the-nation-on-coronavirus-23-march-2020. Accessed 27 August 2023.

———. 2020b. Prime Minister's statement on coronavirus (COVID-19): 16 March 2020. https://www.gov.uk/government/speeches/pm-statement-on-coronavirus-16-march-2020. Accessed 27 August 2023.

Hardie, Andrew. 2014. Modest XML for corpora: Not a standard, but a suggestion. *ICAME Journal* 38 (1): 73–103. https://doi.org/10.2478/icame-2014-0004.

Hunston, Susan. 2022. *Corpora in applied linguistics*. 2nd ed. Cambridge: Cambridge University Press.

Huntley, Selene, J. Michaela Mahlberg, Viola Wiegand, Yves van Gennip, Hui Yang, Rachel S. Dean, and Marnie L. Brennan. 2018. Analysing the opinions of UK veterinarians on practice-based research using corpus linguistic and mathematical methods. *Preventive Veterinary Medicine* 150: 60–69. https://doi.org/10.1016/j.prevetmed.2017.11.020.

Institute for Government. 2020. Timeline of UK government coronavirus lockdowns and restrictions. https://www.instituteforgovernment.org.uk/data-visualisation/timeline-coronavirus-lockdowns. Accessed 27 August 2023.

———. 2022. Timeline of UK government coronavirus lockdown and restrictions. https://www.instituteforgovernment.org.uk/data-visualisation/timeline-coronavirus-lockdowns. Accessed 27 August 2023.

Kilgarrif, Adam, Pavel Rychly, Pavel Smrz, and D. David Tugwell. 2004. The sketch engine. *Proceedings of Euralex* 1: 105–116. https://www.sketchengine.eu/wp-content/uploads/The_Sketch_Engine_2004.pdf. Accessed 27 August 2023.

Kilgarriff, Adam, Vít Baisa, Jan Bušta, Miloš Jakubíček, Vojtěch Kovář, Jan Michelfeit, Pavel Rychlý, and Vít Suchomel. 2014. The sketch engine: Ten years on. *Lexicography* 1: 7–36. https://www.sketchengine.eu/wp-content/uploads/The_Sketch_Engine_2014.pdf. Accessed 27 August 2023.

McClaughlin, Emma, Sara Vilar-Lluch, Tamsin Parnell, Dawn Knight, Elena Nichele, Svenja Adolphs, Jérémie Clos, and Giovanna Schiazza. 2023. The reception of public health messages during the COVID-19 pandemic. *Applied corpus Linguistics* 3 (1). https://doi.org/10.1016/j.acorp.2022.100037.

McEnery, Tony, and Andrew Hardie. 2012. *Corpus linguistics: Method, theory and practice*. Cambridge: Cambridge University Press.

McMenemy, David, Elaine Robinson, and Ian Ruthven. 2023. The impact of COVID-19 lockdowns on public libraries in the UK: Findings from a National Study. *Public Library Quarterly* 42 (1): 92–110.

Northington, Jenn. 2021. Support and hope in the Philadelphia book scene. *Book Riot*, January 13.

Partington, Alan, Alison Duguid, and Charlotte Taylor. 2013. *Patterns and meanings in discourse: Theory and practice in corpus-assisted discourse studies (CADS)*. Amsterdam: John Benjamins.

Saldaña, Johnny. 2011. *Fundamentals of qualitative research*. New York: Oxford University Press.

———. 2021. *The coding manual for qualitative researchers*. 4th ed. Thousand Oak, CA: Sage.

Schmitt, Norbert, and Marianne Cele-Murcia. 2020. An overview of applied linguistics. In *An introduction to applied linguistics*, ed. Norbert Schmitt and Michael P.H. Rodgers, 3rd ed., 1–16. Abingdon: Routledge.

Taylor, Charlotte, and Anna Marchi. 2018. *Corpus approaches to discourse: A critical review*. Abingdon: Routledge.

The Reading Agency. 2020. New survey says reading connects a nation in lockdown. https://readingagency.org.uk/news/media/new-survey-says-reading-connects-a-nation-in-lockdown.html. Accessed 27 August 2023.

Tracy Sarah, J. 2020. *Qualitative research methods: Collecting evidence, crafting analysis, communicating impact*. 2nd ed. Hoboke: John Wiley & Sons.

CHAPTER 2

Reading, Genre, and Crisis

Abstract This chapter surveys the literature on the relationship between pandemics, literature (especially the role played by genre and popular fiction), and reading habits. Drawing on previous studies, we first examine how world pandemics and public health emergencies involving widespread illness have had significant literary and cultural impacts. We specifically examine the relationship of particular genres to times of crisis highlighting how, historically, crisis is manifested often through the production and consumption of genre fiction (as opposed to what might be considered 'literary' fiction), and how there is a long history of readers both confronting anxieties and escaping them through genre fiction. We explore how genre fiction may be a prism through which we can understand contemporary events and provide readers with the distance to work through contemporary anxieties. We then turn to our data by examining the genres that participants in our survey said they read more and those which they said they avoided—and their reasons for doing so. Our analysis demonstrates the relationship between particular genres of literature and the need to cope at a time of crisis.

Keywords Pandemics • Genre • Crisis • Reading

© The Author(s), under exclusive license to Springer Nature Switzerland AG 2024
A. Boucher et al., *Reading Habits in the COVID-19 Pandemic*,
https://doi.org/10.1007/978-3-031-52753-1_2

1   INTRODUCTION

In early 2020, as COVID-19 spread around the globe and national lockdowns became inevitable, news stories (for many people) seemed frantic, sensational, and even apocalyptic. Some of the *least* surprising headlines, however—at least from a literature, film, and genre studies perspective—reported that during this time the most frequently streamed or downloaded entertainment content was apocalyptic or epidemic in nature. Travis Clark, writing for *Business Insider* on 6 March 2020, reported that the then decade-old film *Contagion* (2011) saw its rate of online piracy increase 5609% over the course of January 2020 alone. The film's reinvigorated viewing extended to legitimate channels: at the time of Clark's writing (and as the world approached the skyrocketing likelihood of national lockdowns), *Contagion* was the seventh most popular film downloaded on iTunes while '[e]very other movie in the top 20 was released in 2019'. Remarkably, neither Clark nor any of his interviewees in the article speculated *why* viewers were compelled to return to an older film in such huge numbers. The same day, Heather Kelly writing for *The Washington Post* reported the same figures for *Contagion* but gave more of a rationale for its renewed popularity: that the 'compulsion to watch these fictionalized, sometimes graphic versions of things that are unfolding in the real world can be a way of making sense of what's happening when we're faced with uncertainty'. Within a few weeks, thousands of publications, streaming services, blogs, podcasts, and social media threads began providing recommendation lists of overlooked pandemic films, books, and other media so audiences could lean into this trend—although, like Clark's article, many of these lists did not comment on why this trend had exploded. There seemed to be a collective knowledge that this media was desperately needed by a large audience, but many seemed incapable of articulating why.

These headlines and slews of recommendations for grim entertainment no doubt seemed alarming and strange to many—even to those who found themselves consuming said entertainment against all logic or understanding of their pre-lockdown tastes. From a genre studies perspective, these choices are less confusing. Indeed, for many with training in genre studies, these trends were entirely predictable; as will be explored in the below section on genre fiction and trauma, the irrationality is itself *rational*.

What was far stranger—more than a rise in popularity of bleak entertainment during a bleak moment in history—is the fact that so many outlets reporting on these popularity surges provided next to no explanation for them. Despite actively reporting (usually with an air of surprise) on these genre trends during lockdown, the media generally had very limited engagement with genre reading and its long history with public anxiety in times of crisis. Even more oddly, when there *was* news coverage interrogating why people consumed unlikely genres during the COVID-19 lockdown, it was almost solely relegated to films (and to a lesser extent, television). Despite a vast number of articles discussing the huge uptick in book sales and time spent reading, there was almost no substantial discussion about *what* was being read and *why*. An anonymous author for *BBC Culture* (2020), Kate Knibbs (for *Wired* 2020), and Emma Charlton (for *World Economic Forum* 2020)—all of them writing in late March through late April 2020—note with some surprise the massive rise in book sales, and its impact on small and large bookseller business models, but they only very briefly touch on the actual trends of what's being sold: travel book sales are down, while those for home-based guides like cooking, gardening, and home-schooling are up. The same vagueness continued several months on, out of lockdown: the Editorial Board at the *Financial Times* (2020) was still discussing book sales in very broad and general (rather than *generic*) terms, as was Alison Flood for *The Guardian* (2021), who briefly mentions a few individual book titles with little context for their genre. In October 2020, Nigel Newton, founder and chief executive of Bloomsbury, was quoted saying that:

> people's book choices had reflected the mood of the people throughout the past six months: 'In June we published "Humankind" by Rutger Bregman, people wanted hope and a positive view of humanity, which he gave, and in June itself the biggest social issue of our time, with "Why I'm No Longer Talking to White People about Race"', (Marston 2020)

although the article quickly resumed its focus on sales spikes more broadly. There seemed to be little curiosity about specifics, beyond which extremely broad categories sold well: articles reporting on an increase in reading or book buying often mention a spike in the sale of 'fiction' and rather strangely pass this off as a cohesive, homogenous grouping. That spokespeople for these publishers seemed to have little to report, even from a marketing perspective, on any category narrower than 'fiction' seems an intriguing lacuna in information.

This chapter looks specifically at the survey questions dedicated to forms and genres of reading to gain more specific insight into the texts that the UK public gravitated towards or fled from, and why. More significantly, we pair these survey responses with a greater context about the often-maligned 'genre' and 'popular' fiction (as opposed to 'literary' fiction); we trace the long historical significance of the development genre fiction—which was often produced and consumed in periods of great cultural stress; and we finally tie together more general theories about what purposes genre fiction serve for various audiences, citing our open-text survey responses as evidence. While much genre fiction is understood in hindsight as a consumer response to a period of crisis, this project enables us to see in real-time how readers responded specifically to COVID-19 and the first lockdown through their selection of reading material.

2   Context

2.1   A Definition of 'Genre Fiction'

'Genre fiction'—which is often synonymous with 'popular fiction'—is perhaps best introduced from a marketing perspective: these are rough conceptual categories given to media by creators and distributors to help alert a text's presence to an appropriate audience (the question of audience will become important later). Theoretically, the clearer the genre, the clearer the marketing and promotion of a text can be and the more likely a sale will be made. Broad genres are easily identified and likely spring immediately to mind to the average consumer: horror, comedy, romance, thriller, fantasy, etc. But genres are infinitely granular: the narrower your scope, the more categories and sub-genres there are, and the more overlaps exist among them. The line between thriller and horror, for example, can often blur or fracture. The 'crime fiction' sub-genre of 'thriller' itself produces countless fractals: within crime fiction, would a reader gravitate more towards a whodunnit, a police procedural, a mob or gangster story, true or historical crime, a noir or pulp detective story, a caper or heist, an espionage story, or a courtroom or legal thriller?

One of the most distinctive microgenres in recent decades is even more specific, residing somewhere between a whodunnit, a police procedural, and a noir (and overlapping with categories outside of the 'thriller', such as domestic or feminist drama): what Saner (2015) refers to as the 'female thriller' or 'domestic noir' and what Corrigan (2017) calls the

'Gone-Girl-on-a-Train' genre, named after two of its most popular and defining texts, Gillian Flynn's *Gone Girl* (Flynn 2012) and Paula Hawkins's *Girl on the Train* (Hawkins 2015). The genre is so narrow that it doesn't even have a settled name, and yet it's instantly recognisable and very easy to market: a psychologically fraught thriller bordering on a murder mystery, usually with an unreliable narrator, often set around a domestic or romantic sphere, with a (post-)feminist slant, and typically starring (or victimising) a beautiful, blonde, relatively affluent, white woman dealing with 'millennial jitters [and an] emphasis on character development through therapeutic labeling' (Corrigan 2017). Most of these texts have the word 'girl' in the title, not only to heighten a certain (sometimes ironic) infantilisation of the woman in question, but also to highlight that the authors and anticipated readers are frequently women.

The intended or projected audience is one of the biggest stigmas in defining genre fiction. Schneider-Mayerson articulates that there is no clear definition of popular and genre fiction, apart from it being 'defined by what it's not: "literature"' (2010, p. 22). The problem then becomes: who defines what *is* literature? Literary, cinematic, and artistic criticism has historically been the purview of a small group; for much of history, those who define what 'great art' is, tend to be those who can put monetary value on art and have it designed for them (beginning with wealthy institutions and patrons millennia ago) or those who have access to very high levels of education (usually restricted to wealthy white men, at least for much of Western history). Anything perceived to be written by or for an audience which does not align with the demographics of these tastemakers is often relegated as 'genre' or 'popular' fiction, and thereby contrasted quite starkly with 'literary' fiction. As such, much of the history of literary criticism and the process of defining literary categories is steeped in snobbery, misogyny, racism, and queerphobia, which we see extended well into the twentieth century and beyond: Faber erroneously argues that 'there is not much to be gleaned' from certain types of genre fiction (1971, pp. 12–13), while the literary scholar Victor Neuburg writes that,

> popular literature offers us a window—and it is *certainly no more than this*— upon the world of ordinary men and women [....] Popular literature can be defined as what the *unsophisticated reader has chosen for pleasure*. Such a reader may, of course, come from any class in society, although the primary appeal of popular literature has been the poor – and, by the end of the eighteenth century, also to children. (1977, p. 12, added emphases)

Neuburg's implication that poor people or other readers of popular fiction have the mental faculties of children is directly challenged by Liggins and Duffy, who highlight just how patronising and classist his critique is: 'This [perspective] exposes a number of common misconceptions about popular texts and their readers, namely that the latter are predominantly lower-class, have no critical faculties, and choose texts that have value only as entertainment' (2001, p. xiii). It is an abiding cliche in scholastic and even popular understandings of literature that if a text is written for, or can easily be read or enjoyed by, the masses (i.e. women, children or teenagers, non-white people, lower-class people, or queer people, among just a few), then it cannot have artistic merit. To return briefly to the 'Gone-Girl-on-a-Train' genre, part of the genre's popularity stems from a critical misalignment based on this cliché: 'Gone-Girl-on-a-Train' novels integrate 'highbrow,' 'literary' aspects into genre fiction that is written largely by and for women, a combination which surprised and confused many reviewers. Miller, writing for *Salon*, said that the 'bar is not necessarily high' for crime fiction but that *Gone Girl* 'kick[ed] the genre into a higher gear [and] might have been written by Jonathan Franzen or Jeffrey Eugenides [rather than] Flynn, a former staff writer for Entertainment Weekly [sic],' ending the article saying this is emphatically *not* 'a literary novel in disguise' but that it is somehow equal parts 'literary' novel and genre fiction (Miller 2012). It is not difficult to parse Miller's rhetoric, which separates out the highbrow (written by intellectual men) and the lowbrow (written by women with connections to the entertainment industry) and to see the direct influence of Neuburg, Faber, and other critics on these continuing literary segregations.

In fairness to those who have censured it for its supposed formulaic nature or economically mercenary functions, genre fiction can sometimes be a victim of its own success. As genre and popular fiction does not often *critically* thrive due to its qualitatively 'lesser' (if quantitatively large) target audiences, genre fiction is most often valued from a purely commercial standpoint. When a fresh genre or voice breaks through into both the critical and popular realms, publishers commission a slew of copycats, often to diminishing returns and rote distillations, and all entries within that genre are then tarred with the same brush regardless of quality. But this formula-writing practice is, in itself, intriguing, especially as it concerns audience reception. We would add to Liggins and Duffy's rebuttal of Neuburg and their praise of genre fiction—as we will see in the below study—that the role of pleasure, of catharsis, or of safety through generic formula is not only extraordinarily important to our critical understandings of how literature works but also that these feelings of pleasure, catharsis, or safety can often be sophisticatedly and intentionally wrought by authors, complexly understood by readers, and of great benefit to the public's mental health. Indeed, our survey provides a great deal of evidence to that point: many of the open-text responses provided thoughtful and critical introspection about the responders' genre-reading practices and the benefits that readers gained. Further, and as will be seen fully in the next section, genre and popular fiction has a robust history heavily tied to cultural trauma and anxiety. It is to do a great disservice to readers, writers, and the history of print culture to give an outright dismissal of genre fiction's cultural, historical, artistic, and (especially as it concerns this study) healthcare importance.

2.2 Trauma and Genre Fiction Studies: A Historical Overview

Drawing on previous studies, this section surveys the relationship between historical periods of crises and the concurrent development of genre and popular fiction. Artwork and other creative practices—which are always reflections of those who consume them and the time in which they are created—have always reflected or responded to periods of anxiety. However, there were several restrictions throughout much of history about how the *form* and *genre* of literature could acknowledge new social developments or anxieties. Narrative fiction before the rise of the novel was generically very limited: plays were classically divided into three categories (comedy, tragedy, and history), all with their own strict rules and conventions, while narrative poetry had its own formal distinctions. The novel—a new form of writing, independent from previous artistic restrictions—took off in Europe in the late seventeenth and early eighteenth centuries, and with it came a freedom to explore new genres and to relay stories to an audience in new ways. While there are many conditions which led to the rise of the novel and its many new genres beyond 'comedy', 'tragedy', and 'history', some of the more intriguing genres are those whose development and popularity are more *explicitly* constructed around moments of profound social stress and dilemma. In these examples, as will be seen, genre itself operates as a sort of safety valve for public emotion. A highly abridged history of the connection between genre fiction and its direct correlation to trauma will provide necessary context for the findings of our study on reading habits during the lockdown.

Gothic fiction is perhaps the genre with the lineage most clearly rooted in social anxiety, especially considering its constant resurgences in popularity during times of social strain. It crystalised as a genre in the late eighteenth century not only as a cultural response against the cool rationality of Enlightenment thinkers but also as a response to the horrors of the French Revolution, to the instability of several other surviving monarchies, and to various religious wars: the Marquis de Sade found the Gothic novel to be the most natural, predictable consequence for revolutionary sentiment in Europe (Sade 2005, pp. 3–20). The genre's focus on polluted or uncertain family lineages was a direct reaction to new scientific disciplines like archaeology, geology, and antiquarianism which had begun to query human genesis, the roots of social and class behaviour, and the validity of religious origin stories and eschatology. Ellis writes in his *History of Gothic Fiction* that the genre is more than just a reaction to anxieties about history and modernity; it 'is itself a theory of history: a mode for the apprehension and consumption of history', in which the form and structures of the genre cannot be separated from the anxieties it comments on (Ellis 2000, p. 11). Characterised by its use of violence, taboo sexuality, the sublime, and the supernatural, it was a site of major formal experimentation which emphasised its ability to unnerve readers and to transform what was safe and known into a source of wonder and anxiety. In a 1774 essay, Aiken explained the irrational popularity of this genre as a 'paradox of the heart', in which the negative feelings that Gothic fiction provokes in a reader (fear, dread, disgust) are somehow transformed into positive feelings (delight, relief, excitement) (Aiken and Aiken 1774, p. 57). These transhistorical illogical emotional responses would keep the Gothic popular until the present day and account for major financial successes of horror films. These counterintuitive reactions would also be responsible for lockdown readers and viewers gravitating towards pandemic-themed media that emphasised their own fears and uncertainty.

While the Gothic leaned into maladjusted, exploitative plots and structures to represent a maladjusted, exploitative world, other genres responded with equal enthusiasm but more ambiguity about the conditions of their own development. Sensation fiction, which was enormously popular in the middle of the nineteenth century, was characterised by its tendency towards domestic melodrama, mixed with greater and more salacious social problems, crime stories, early psychology, and a general collapsing of traditional boundaries among social demographics, landscapes, and even time. Significantly, the genre itself often seemed unsure of its own stance towards these fluctuations, but it became a special 'target of [critical] attack because it represented the entry into middle-class publishing institutions of the sensationalism that characterized the working-class literature of the preceding decades' (Cvetkovich 1992, pp. 15–16). The genre's very existence was an uneasy product of the disintegrating social boundaries paradoxically fretted over in its pages. For readers, the equivocating stance of the genre was itself a draw: there was a therapeutic element to addressing major concerns without forcing a conclusive worldview on a reader; for many, it was enough to explore different vantages and perspectives about a world in upheaval, simply—as the genre's title implies—to *feel* something. This sought experience, to explore ambiguous feelings and trauma responses from a moderate perspective, will be seen in our dataset.

Some readers preferred an even *more* tempered middle ground than what sensation fiction provided—one which relied on *not* feeling. Detective fiction was one of the most frequently cited genres in our data set; much like Gothic literature which constantly reinvents itself and has never fallen out of fashion since its inception, detective fiction is a similarly transhistorical response to crisis periods. While detective fiction had the same nineteenth-century origins as sensation fiction—namely the creeping dread of modernity and the growing ambiguity in the categorisation of the world—detective fiction bifurcated from its mother-genre to explore these issues in a different form and for a different psychological purpose. Rather than leaning into ambiguity and uncertainty like the somewhat experimental sensation fiction does, detective fiction manufactures chaos purely so it can show ordered restored at the end of the narrative: what Wyndham called 'animated algebra' (Wyndham 1975, p. 1078), a place where logic prevails. Despite the often grisly and Gothic content of these texts, detective fiction underscores (rather than undermines) a sense of structural safety. This focus on strict rules and conventions—with guild-sanctioned guidelines such as Knox's '10 Commandments of Detective Fiction' (1929) and Van Dine's 'Twenty Rules for Writing Detective Stories' (1928)—enables a reader to understand that prurient, macabre, and distressing situations can be confined in knowable, rational generic structures and can therefore be safely accessed. Predictability in reading material will prove to be an enduringly popular mental health outlet, as will be seen in the below analysis and discussed further in Chaps. 3, 5, and 6.

Not everyone is keen to use literature as a safety valve *at all*, though. As will be seen in our data set, one of the more frequent types of narratives that attracted readers during the lockdown was anything 'light' or 'escapist' or with an 'HEA' (i.e. 'happily ever after' ending): fantasy, romance, certain types of historical novels, cheerful adventure stories. These stories, which have their roots in several historical genres (utopian fiction, comedy, literature of sensibility, melodrama, Ruritanian fiction, fantasy, the romance) are example of an audience's need to opt out and to embed themselves in worlds which contemporaneous threats simply cannot permeate (Boucher 2023).

3 Methodology

The data in this chapter are drawn specifically from Questions 11.i–11.iv, 15–17, and 21–23 of the *Aston Lockdown Reading Survey Corpus* and provide as full a portrait as possible of readers' genre preferences and avoidances both before lockdown and then during lockdown; questions about preferred or avoided *forms* of fiction go beyond the remit of this chapter. As the questions we asked participants offered them a range of ways to answer, we will subsequently use a variety of methodological approaches for analysis. These methods include a more quantitative presentation for the questions that generated numerical data, as well as a larger qualitative analysis of questions with free-text responses.

For example, Questions 11.i–11.iv asked participants to rank a statement about their genre preferences or avoidances on a scale from 'strongly agree' to 'strongly disagree'; this numerical data will be presented in bar graph form below. Questions 15, 16, 21, and 22 asked participants to tick all of the relevant genres which applied to them, from the following list in terms of their preferences and avoidances, both before and then during lockdown:

- Action and adventure
- Children's literature
- Classic and realist literature
- Comedy and satire
- Detective and crime fiction
- Fairy tales
- Fantasy
- Historical fiction
- Horror and Gothic fiction
- Myths, fables, legends

- Post-apocalyptic fiction
- Romance
- Science and speculative fiction
- Thriller
- Other

These genres were carefully selected and tailored during survey design to cover the most ground possible (often in line with how booksellers market and segregate different genres, as those would be familiar categories to participants), while also avoiding being too granular. Minute specificity would make analysing data very difficult, even assuming a participant would be able to make it through a thoroughly exhaustive list of all subgenres. For our four tick-boxing questions on genre, there was no limit on how many genres participants could select for each question. The data generated are presented numerically in across the analysis sections. Questions 17 and 23 generated free-text responses and form two sub-corpora of 9330 and 6296 tokens respectively. The responses to these questions were inductively coded to identify emerging thematic patterns; these themes form the basis of our additional analysis in Sects. 4.3 and 4.4.

4 ANALYSIS

4.1 Genre Preferences Before Lockdown

Question 11.i asked participants to rank the accuracy of the statement, 'Before the lockdown, I was drawn to particular forms or genres'. This question was designed to introduce a sense of self-reflection in the participant about their reading habits. Significantly, this question also strived to give researchers a baseline for how participants *perceived* or *remembered* their reading habits to be.[1] Responses to this question are displayed in Table 2.1:

Based on these results, most of our participants were seemingly aware that they had certain established genre fiction preferences. When it came

---

[1] As with all reflections and self-perceptions, there is the possibility that these are skewed or perhaps inaccurate to the actual practice of genre selection.

Table 2.1 Summary of responses to Question 11.i

Option	Number and percentage of responses selecting option
Strongly agree	249 (29%)
Agree	416 (48.4%)
Neither agree nor disagree	124 (14.4%)
Disagree	66 (7.7%)
Strongly disagree	4 (0.5%)

Table 2.2 Summary of responses to Question 15

Option	Number and percentage of responses selecting option
Action and adventure	231 (27.1%)
Children's literature	187 (22%)
Classic and realist literature	524 (61.6%)
Comedy and satire	277 (32.5%)
Detective and crime fiction	508 (59.7%)
Fairy tales	91 (10.7%)
Fantasy	316 (37.1%)
Historical fiction	446 (52.4%)
Horror and Gothic fiction	189 (22.2%)
Myths, fables, legends	183 (21.5%)
Post-apocalyptic fiction	237 (27.8%)
Romance	251 (29.5%)
Science and speculative fiction	281 (33%)
Thriller	305 (35.8%)
Other	88 (10.3%)

to allowing them to expound on what those pre-lockdown preferences were, Question 15 asked, 'Before the lockdown, which genres of fiction did you prefer to read?' Responses to this question are displayed in Table 2.2. This was a multi-answer question, so participants were able to select more than one option.[2]

Table 2.2 highlights that the highest scoring genres were 'Classic and realist literature', followed by 'Detective and crime fiction' and 'Historical fiction'. The lowest scoring genre was 'Fairy tales'. Everything else scored between 20% and 40%.

---

[2] Consequently for this question, and similar multi-answer questions here and elsewhere in the book, single percentages for each option do not add up to 100% in total.

4.2 Genre Avoidances Before Lockdown

Preferences are not enough to get a baseline portrait; we also needed to account for avoidances. In Question 11.iii, we asked 'Before the lockdown, I avoided particular forms or genres'. The responses to this question are displayed in Table 2.3.

In Question 21, we then gave participants space to list what those pre-lockdown avoidances were, as displayed in Table 2.4.

Table 2.3 Summary of responses to Question 11.iii

Option	Number and percentage of responses selecting option
Strongly agree	194 (22.6%)
Agree	393 (45.8%)
Neither agree nor disagree	134 (15.6%)
Disagree	116 (13.5%)
Strongly disagree	22 (2.6%)

Table 2.4 Summary of responses to Question 21

Option	Number and percentage of responses selecting option
Action and adventure	220 (28.5%)
Children's literature	228 (29.6%)
Classic and realist literature	110 (14.3%)
Comedy and satire	135 (17.5%)
Detective and crime fiction	125 (16.2%)
Fairy tales	271 (35.1%)
Fantasy	301 (39%)
Historical fiction	136 (17.6%)
Horror and Gothic fiction	399 (51.8%)
Myths, fables, legends	214 (27.8%)
Post-apocalyptic fiction	309 (40.1%)
Romance	332 (43.1%)
Science and speculative fiction	308 (39.9%)
Thriller	223 (28.9%)
Other	13 (1.7%)

The top scoring genre for pre-lockdown avoidances was 'Horror and Gothic fiction', followed by four other closely scoring genres: Romance, Post-apocalyptic fiction, Science and speculative fiction, and Fantasy. These results roughly align with (and as the inverse of) trends seen in the pre-lockdown preferences section and begin to create a baseline for the normal reading habits of our participants.

4.3 Genre Preferences During Lockdown

We now examine how participants reported how reading habits had changed during/since lockdown. Question 11.ii asked, 'Since the start of the lockdown, I have been drawn to particular forms and genres'. This question was written to help participants begin to identify any shifts in patterns and preferences (or to note a lack of change) and begin thinking about why such shifts were or were not taking place. Responses are shown in Table 2.5. Participant answers indicated that, generally, they were slightly less drawn to any specific genres during lockdown than they had been before the pandemic.

This lessening of certainty about genre preference is intriguing, as will become more apparent in the paragraph below, in our discussion of the free-text answers for Question 17. Participants will later describe in very assured ways what their genre preferences were during lockdown. In that later section, few participants indicated that they were indifferent to what genre they read (let alone the combined 31.3% of participants who neither agreed nor disagreed, disagreed, or strongly disagreed in Question 11.ii). While most participants eventually reported very strong preferences, nearly a third of participants seemed loath to admit it until they could introduce specifics in their own words. We will discuss this in more depth in a later section, although it is worth noting here. This tonal shift between

Table 2.5 Summary of responses to Question 11.ii

Option	Number and percentage of responses selecting option
Strongly agree	236 (27.5%)
Agree	355 (41.3%)
Neither agree nor disagree	168 (19.6%)
Disagree	90 (10.5%)
Strongly disagree	10 (1.2%)

answers could potentially be the general perception of security and certainty in pre-lockdown life. With so many elements of life in flux during the time participants were responding to the survey, it is possible that readers overestimated their assuredness of genre preference before lockdown or underestimated it during the unmooring environment of lockdown. It is also possible that the open text boxes enabled participants to work through their preferences more therapeutically and therefore land on a more confident or definitive assessment of their preferences than a tick-box answer allowed them to do.

Question 16 asked readers to indicate which genres they have preferred reading since lockdown started. Results are in Table 2.6.

The highest scoring genres were the same as the pre-lockdown genres, although none scored quite as highly as they did before lockdown (the highest scorers dropped in popularity from about 7–13%). While participants once again listed Fairy tales as the lowest scoring genre (dropping a further 2.3%), it should be noted that several other genres dipped significantly in popularity, with its percentages now reaching the teens.

Strangely, *every* genre dipped in popularity; only Children's literature and Romance stayed within one percentage point of their pre-lockdown figures, although they *did* still have a slight dip. The data reveal that

Table 2.6 Summary of responses to Question 16

Option	Number and percentage of responses selecting option
Action and adventure	184 (21.9%)
Children's literature	183 (21.8%)
Classic and realist literature	411 (48.9%)
Comedy and satire	251 (29.8%)
Detective and crime fiction	425 (50.5%)
Fairy tales	71 (8.4%)
Fantasy	264 (31.4%)
Historical fiction	377 (44.8%)
Horror and Gothic fiction	142 (16.9%)
Myths, fables, legends	142 (16.9%)
Post-apocalyptic fiction	145 (17.2%)
Romance	245 (21.1%)
Science and speculative fiction	221 (26.3%)
Thriller	213 (25.3%)
Other	89 (10.6%)

people believed they were gravitating towards genre fiction (even including 'literary fiction') far less than they had been before lockdown; perhaps this may be explained via an overlap with a general shift away from reading at all (see Chap. 3 for longer discussions on how commuting, caring responsibilities, and mental health concerns—among just a few issues—impacted the time our participants spent reading).

In Question 17, we asked, 'If you have been drawn to particular genres during the lockdown period, why do you think this is the case?' As will be seen again in Chaps. 3 and 6, free-text answers tended to elicit metaphorical or themed responses from participants. We group the responses to Question 17 into the following categories: 'Escape', 'Catharsis and Learning', 'Security and Familiarity'. These are similar, but not identical, to some of the metaphorical or thematic categories seen in Chaps. 3 and 6.

4.3.1 Escape

Frequently occurring words in all sections are 'escapism' and 'escapist'—this is perhaps the most notable feature of the data set. For example, 'I didn't want to read heavy, complex books', reports Participant 86, as they 'Couldn't focus'. However, most of these responses were less about gravitating *towards* a light and happy genre and framed more as an *avoidance* of other genres. As this exact question about avoidance is asked of participants later, we will address this issue in the relevant below section. Although participants did not necessarily answer the question being asked here, it is still intriguing that they occasionally struggled to differentiate the idea of preferences and avoidances. The 'happily ever after' escapists were not drawn necessarily to these books in their own right but out of anxiety felt for some other genres; these choices of texts were seemingly made from a lack of other options that the reader could mentally handle in the lockdown period.

4.3.2 Catharsis and Learning

There were a number of other participants who (much like with readers of Gothic and sensation fiction during their initial heyday) leaned into darker genres 'because this situation may be bad [but] I want to read worse' (Participant 481). Those who are drawn to darker content found that it 'Breaks the normal mundane and get[s me] a quick buzz of adrenaline' or is 'Clearly [...] some sort of stress mechanism?' (Participant 512). Participant 49 said of their new lockdown preferences, 'Reading about pandemics in post apocalyptic [sic] fiction feels kind of therapeutic in our current circumstance'. Another (Participant 98) reports, 'Post-apocalyptic fiction is a genre I've always like [sic] but I thought it would unsettle me now. Actually I've been more drawn to it'. The draw is perhaps easy to explain: horror film scholar Lindsey Decker says of genre fiction in relation to the pandemic,

> One of the great things about horror is it allows us to experience heightened emotions. We can experience fear and tension and suspense, but we have control over it [....] We can hit pause any time we want – we can fast forward. We have control over our experience of that fear, which I think is very comforting. (Kelly 2020)

Participant 109 said they enjoyed the 'variety' of dystopian texts, while several others indicated a potential learning outcome from reading dystopian fiction: it allows them 'to compare situations' (Participant 156) and acknowledge the benefits of 'Visiting other periods of history which had pandemics' (Participant 425). Participant 209, opposing the escapism of happier genres, found a deeper emotional resonance provided by dystopian, post-apocalyptic, or science-fiction stories, writing that they could 'identify more with the stories about being inside a spaceship for months at a time, interacting with a limited group of people'.

4.3.3 Security and Familiarity

Some readers found security in books with clear patterns and expected outcomes, for example:

> I've found myself wanting to read stories where a good person triumphs over evoke [sic] or chaos in a relatively recognisable world – eg thrillers etc. I commented that it's escapist almost like superhero conics [sic] during the Second World War, the reassurance that the good guys can win. (Participant 120)

One participant neatly summarised their genre rationale in a handy equation: 'Familiarity = Comfort and Control' (Participant 358). Despite the gruesome content and novel situations of many mysteries and detective stories, the genre still had the potential to remind readers 'of the normalcy of pre-pandemic life' (Participant 389), perhaps not through the content but through the formal devices which are often highly regulated and familiar: 'Crime novels have a familiar cast of characters; danger etc at a distance; and satisfactory endings' (Participant 451); 'Romance and

Mystery offer closure and a guarantee of either a Happily Ever After or Justice. Both are enormously comforting during this time' (Participant 475). Ideas of security from reading will gain further resonance in Chap. 3, 5, and 6.

4.4 Genre Avoidances During Lockdown

Despite this question being half-answered in many of the open text boxes of the previous section about lockdown preferences, we gave participants a chance to talk more explicitly about genres of fiction they found themselves actively avoiding since lockdown. Question 11.iv asked, 'Since the start of the lockdown, I have been avoiding particular forms of genres'. The responses are illustrated in Table 2.7.

Much as when participants indicated that they were less *drawn* to particular genres during the lockdown, here participants say they also avoided certain genres *less* than they did before the pandemic (with all answers evening out and shifting more towards apathy by between 1.5% and 5%).

Regardless of this growing pattern of indifference, in which our participants indicated that they now cared less what they read or don't read, both the genre-specific tick boxes and the open textbox responses will tell a different story. In Question 22, we asked participants to tell us which genres they now avoided reading. The results are in Table 2.8.

The topmost avoided genre was again Horror and Gothic fiction (as it had been pre-lockdown), but the second most avoided genre was Post-apocalyptic fiction (up 12.2% from before lockdown), which wildly upset the previously number-two most avoided genre, Romance (whose avoidance *fell* 6.9%). All other genre categories stayed relatively stable from their pre-lockdown avoidance figures.

Table 2.7 Summary of responses to Question 11.iv

Option	Number and percentage of responses selecting option
Strongly agree	178 (20.7%)
Agree	349 (40.6%)
Neither agree nor disagree	159 (18.5%)
Disagree	139 (16.2%)
Strongly disagree	34 (4%)

Table 2.8 Summary of responses to Question 22

Option	Number and percentage of responses selecting option
Action and adventure	218 (28.2%)
Children's literature	223 (28.8%)
Classic and realist literature	136 (17.6%)
Comedy and satire	126 (16.3%)
Detective and crime fiction	136 (17.6%)
Fairy tales	274 (35.4%)
Fantasy	373 (35.3%)
Historical fiction	141 (18.2%)
Horror and Gothic fiction	418 (54.1%)
Myths, fables, legends	213 (27.6%)
Post-apocalyptic fiction	404 (52.3%)
Romance	280 (36.2%)
Science and speculative fiction	325 (42%)
Thriller	234 (30.3%)
Other	15 (1.9%)

The disparity between how people conceptualise their broad, general avoidance in simple terms, and how they articulated their avoidance, only grows in the free-text responses of Question 23, which asked, 'If you have been avoiding particular genres during the lockdown period, why do you think this is the case?' Participants often had very strong tastes in this regard and little hesitancy in expressing those tastes, even in categories where it wasn't explicitly asked for. As previously discussed, participants often struggled to divorce their current reading likes from their current dislikes. Robust preferences and avoidances appear all over the survey and we will see similar patterns emerging in this section that we saw in the last. Once again, the free-text responses showed significant metaphorical or thematic patterns, which will be grouped as follows: 'Fear of Proximity and Mental Health', 'Escape', and 'Complicity'.

4.4.1 Fear of Proximity and Mental Health

Participants frequently used the metaphor of certain darker genres being 'too close for comfort' or 'too close to home'. This is an intriguing turn of phrase, given much of the discourse during the lockdown about comfort and staying close to home. The sheer volume of participants who used this metaphorical phrase may go beyond its status as a common idiom and could perhaps speak to the sense of claustrophobia and sense of invasion prevalent in the culture. The metaphor certainly extended to reading preferences, as well as readers' articulation of those preferences. Participants began to speak more explicitly about mental health concerns, expressing which genres or topics they 'couldn't bear' (Participant 277), which 'heightens anxiety' (Participant 56), or which would give 'difficult to shake off uncomfortable feelings in lockdown [when I] am emotionally exhausted' (Participant 124). Participant 103 only responded with 'Looking after my mental health', with their mental health's connection to reading only being vaguely implied but perceived to be self-evident. The length of a book—which can, in part, be a feature of a genre—was also a determining feature in terms of mental health. Many cited preferring shorter, lighter works for the sake of novelty, compromised attention span, and because there was less pressure of commitment: '"important" [i.e. literary or canonical] books are too challenging atm [at the moment]' (Participant 253).

4.4.2 Escape

There was also a blending of these two categories in which both the fearful 'proximity' of a genre overlapped with issues of mental health to create a slightly separate issue (greater than the sum of its parts) about cognition and its role in 'escape'. A reader's inability to focus on and immerse themselves in other worlds—for whatever reason—contributed to genre avoidance. The fog of mental health concerns meant many participants lacked the focus to fully succumb to fictional worlds, being jarred instead back into non-fictional struggles. Many cited that they felt they already lived in a dystopia and there was therefore a difficulty in certain types of escapism when a fictional world blended too strongly with their perceptions of the real world: Post-apocalyptic fiction was 'Too close to reality, at present [and] too many scenarios from novels [are] ringing true' (Participant 409); 'Since we're living through an apocalypse, I don't need to read about it' (Participant 478). One participant (Participant 234) viewed reading on more moralistic or citizenship terms, in which escaping to another world was a slight abdication of responsibility: 'I want to focus on […] the difficulties and political problems rather than distract myself with fantasy escapism…', a comment made all the more interesting for ending on an ellipses in which the sentence drifts off into an imaginative, unsaid ending, rather than concluding definitively.[3]

---

[3] See also our discussion of 'ESCAPE' in Chap. 5.

4.4.3 Complicity

There was only a very slight increase in participants saying they avoided detective and mystery fiction and, as we saw before, a very large increase in participants gravitating towards that genre, due to the safety of its rules and formulae. That said, a small number of participants alluded to avoiding detective and mystery fiction due to another moment of international anxiety, beyond the pandemic and lockdown: the Black Lives Matter (BLM) protests which took place around the world through the spring and summer of 2020. A great number of participants indicated in the 'Other' field for questions about genre preferences or in the free-text boxes that they had recently been attracted to reading books about critical race theory and/or by Black authors; this, of course, was not mentioned in earlier sections as we asked questions about genres of fiction, rather than about non-fiction (like critical race theory and philosophy, or about the ethno-racial backgrounds of authors). This seemingly tangential thread of preferences takes on new traction in the 'genre avoidance' questions, however: several participants said they had begun avoiding detective fiction to avoid any sense of tacit approval in policing structures. For example, Participant 395 reported,

> More of a correlation than a causation, but I've been avoiding police/detective stories since the major police riots and extreme police brutality happening since the BLM protests started in May. The police system is so corrupt that police/detective stories leave a sour taste now.

In this instance, the familiarity and perceived safety of the detective story structure took on a different resonance, reflecting to this participant some of the structural inequalities and routine injustices they perceived in the policing system. This is a fresh and unusual perspective about genre fiction, in which texts with well-established rules are either viewed as dull, cheap, and unoriginal *or* as a refuge and source of comfort. This reader here finds different structural significance in the building blocks of the genre itself, which (as discussed above with the 'Gone-Girl-on-a-Train' genre) can often absorb, reflect, and perpetuate the conditions of the world in which the genres were created.

Much like with the section before about lockdown preferences, participants had a hard time separating out what they were consciously avoiding from what they were seeking. Many of our answers in these two sections were therefore neat overlaps or complements of each other and it was occasionally tempting to consolidate the two open text sections and consider them as one large data pool. However, considering them separately, despite clear overlaps, enabled us to see what participants *avoided* saying in the other question. When asked directly what they liked, many participants talked about what they avoided. When asked what they avoided, many participants talked about what they liked, which in itself is worth noting, if that's how participants approached their responses.

5 Conclusion

As we highlighted in Sect. 1, there is a long history of readers both confronting and escaping contemporary anxieties through the clear boundaries and reasonably expected ingredients of particular genres—promises which cannot be made to an audience through the fuzzier marketing, formulae, and features of 'literary' fiction. It is likely still too early to determine exactly what new fiction genres may emerge from this particular period of crisis.[4] It *is* likely, however, that over the coming years we may see media with novel emphases, tones, or structures amounting to new or reinvigorated genre fiction. What we can determine thus far, though, is what older, established genre fiction found new use for readers during the first lockdown.

There were intriguing disparities in our survey responses. A greater percentage of our participants claimed that during lockdown they were much more apathetic about what they read, that they had fewer preferences or avoidances than they did before, that genre fiction, seemingly, didn't matter as much anymore. This self-reflection was then undone with more specific questions, in which participants showed that the popularity for *all* genres went down *and* that there were some very clear, strong genres being avoided. Participants were seemingly right that their reading preferences became more ambivalent during lockdown (and this may be complicated by other factors which decrease the desire to read at all, like having less time to read or a shorter attention span). However, participants were certainly contradictory in their opinion that they also didn't avoid any genres in particular: they were remarkably clear in subsequent questions that they had strong avoidances.

Those two had particular avoidances and preferences in their reading material during the lockdown separated generally into two camps: the first

---

[4] See, however, Giovanelli (2022), who discusses the emerging genre of 'Covid poetry'.

camp wanted to confront the pandemic head-on and chose darker reading material as a sort of safety valve through which they could process current emotions; they leaned towards horror, post-apocalyptic, dystopia, Gothic, and science-fiction texts. The second camp sought escapism from current fears and instead chose lighter reading fare, often with an 'HEA' (happily ever after); they leaned towards romance, historical fiction, comedy, children's literature, fantasy, fairy tales, or myths, fables, and legends. The second camp seemingly far outweighed the first: more people found relief and release by removing themselves entirely from real-world anxieties, rather than catharsis through facing them. However, this division of camps is not as clear as it looks. Two categories, detective and crime fiction and thrillers, complicate these numbers through their generic mechanisms. There are two competing factors with detective fiction and thrillers: dark and grim content, regulated by the perceived safety of a strict and knowable formula in which logic prevails. It is this blending of bleak subject matters with a sort of HEA escapism which makes the popularity of detective fiction and thrillers difficult to categorise: which camp do these genres fall into, and what, therefore, are the real numbers in the division between the two camps of reading? There were participants from both sides who considered detective fiction and thrillers to be in their remit, and participants from both sides who considered the genres to be in the other camp's remit. What's more interesting, rather than trying to shoehorn some conceptually complex genres into one camp or the other, is that these genres work as a bridge between the two camps and illustrates the complicated and manifold psychological needs that genre fiction can fulfil during a time of great social stress.

Genre fiction is a prism through which we can understand contemporary events and can provide readers with the mental distance to work through contemporary anxieties, either through avoidance, confrontation, or some other psychological device. Our research illustrates that although readers often have contradictory understandings of their own reading habits, they have a much greater grasp on their own emotional and cognitive needs. It is through repeated questioning and through approaching the subject from different and open angles that readers begin to unpack their reading habits and generic preferences more thoroughly.

References

Aiken, John, and Anna Laetitia Aiken. 1774. On the pleasure derived from objects of terror. In *Miscellaneous pieces in prose*, 57–65. Belfast: James Agee.

Anonymous. 2020. Coronavirus: Book sales surge as readers seek escapism and education. *BBC Culture*, March 26. https://www.bbc.co.uk/news/entertainment-arts-52048582. Accessed 4 May 2023.

Boucher, Abigail. 2023. *Science, medicine, and aristocratic lineage in Victorian popular fiction*. London: Palgrave Macmillan.

Charlton, Emma. 2020. Coronavirus escapism: book sales surge during lockdown. *World Economic Forum*, April 30. https://www.weforum.org/agenda/2020/04/coronavirus-escapism-book-sales-surge-covid-19/. Accessed 4 May 2023.

Clark, Travis. 2020. Pandemic movie "Contagion" [sic] is surging in popularity due to the coronavirus and has hit the No. 7 spot on iTunes, *Business Insider*, March 6. https://www.businessinsider.com/coronavirus-contagion-movie-is-surging-in-piracy-rentals-on-itunes-2020-3?r=US&IR=T. Accessed 4 May 2023.

Corrigan, Maureen. 2017. What "Gone Girl" and "The Girl on the Train" have wrought, *The Washington Post*, January 11. https://www.washingtonpost.com/entertainment/books/what-gone-girl-and-the-girl-on-the-train-have-wrought/2017/01/11/33dcf838-d114-11e6-9cb0-54ab630851e8_story.html. Accessed 4 May 2023.

Cvetkovich, Ann. 1992. *Mixed feelings: Feminism, mass culture, and Victorian sensationalism*. New Brunswick, NJ: Rutgers University Press.

Editorial Board. 2020. Books prove an escapist pleasure in lockdown, *The Financial Times*, October 30. https://www.ft.com/content/62a4d171-ec81-4056-a677-a23ee6956f74. Accessed 4 May 2023.

Ellis, Markman. 2000. *The history of gothic fiction*. Edinburgh: Edinburgh University Press.

Faber, Richard. 1971. *Proper stations: Class in Victorian fiction*. London: Faber and Faber.

Flood, Alison. 2021. 'Book Sales defy pandemic to hit eight-year high', *The Guardian*, January 25. https://www.theguardian.com/books/2021/jan/25/bookshops-defy-pandemic-to-record-highest-sales-for-eight-years#:~:text=More%20than%20200m%20print%20books,book%20sales%20monitor%20Nielsen%20BookScan. Accessed 4 May 2023.

Flynn, Gillian. 2012. *Gone Girl*. New York: Crown Publishing Group.

Giovanelli, Marcello. 2022. Reading the lockdown: Responding to covid poetry. *Journal of Poetry Therapy* 36: 210–225.

Hawkins, Paula. 2015. *The girl on the train*. New York: Riverhead Publishing.

Kelly, Heather. 2020. People have found a way to cope with pandemic fears: Watching "Contagion". *The Washington Post*, March 6. https://www.washingtonpost.com/technology/2020/03/06/contagion-streaming/. Accessed 4 May 2023.
Knibbs, Kate. 2020. The Coronavirus Pandemic Is Changing How People Buy Books. *Wired*, April 27. https://www.wired.com/story/coronavirus-book-sales-indie/. Accessed 4 May 2023.
Knox, Ronald. 1929. Introduction. In *The best [English] detective stories of 1928*. London: Faber. [n.p.].
Liggins, Emma, and Daniel Duffy. 2001. Introduction. In *Feminist readings of Victorian popular texts: Divergent femininities*, ed. Emma Liggins and Daniel Duffy, xiii–xxiv. Aldershot: Ashgate.
Marston, Rebecca. 2020. Coronavirus: People "rediscovering books" as lockdown sales jump. *BBC Business*, October 27. https://www.bbc.co.uk/news/business-54703164. Accessed 4 May 2023.
Miller, Laura. 2012. "Gone Girl": Marriage can be murder. *Salon*, June 4. https://www.salon.com/2012/06/04/gone_girl_marriage_can_be_murder/. Accessed 10 May 2023.
Neuburg, Victor E. 1977. *Popular literature: A history and guide from the beginning of printing to the year 1897*. London: The Woburn Press.
Sade, Marquis de. 2005. [1800]. An essay on novels. In *The crimes of love*, ed. trans. David Coward, 3–20. Oxford: Oxford University Press.
Saner, Emine. 2015. The Girl on the Train: how Paula Hawkins wrote "the new Gone Girl". *The Guardian*, April 21. https://www.theguardian.com/books/2015/apr/21/the-girl-on-the-train-paula-hawkins-new-gone-girl-female-thriller-authors-gillian-flynn. Accessed 4 May 2023.
Schneider-Mayerson, Matthew. 2010. Popular fiction studies: The advantages of a new field. *Studies in Popular Culture* 33 (1): 21–35.
Van Dine, S. S. [Willard Huntington Wright]. 1928. Twenty Rules for Writing Detective Stories. *The American Magazine* (September).
Wyndham, Francis. 1975. Animated Algebra. *The Times Literary Supplement*, September 26. 1078.

CHAPTER 3

Reading and Time

Abstract This chapter examines how participants reported that the lockdown period had affected the amount that they read. We begin by providing an overview of the likely effect of lockdown on participants' time, for example, in the reduction of commuting and the increase in home working and home-schooling children, both of which may have impacted on time that was previously used for reading or may have, conversely, provided opportunities for reading that did not previously exist. We then turn to our data to focus on two key findings. First, we examine how participants reported the effect of gaining or losing time on the amount they read (more or less than pre-pandemic). Second, we look at how our participants perceived their use of time and their use of particular metaphors to frame their understanding of time related to the quality and quantity of their reading. Here we examine how reading itself is often personified and presented as an agentive figure acting on the reader through time.

Keywords Time • Reading frequency • Metaphor • Agency

1 INTRODUCTION

In this chapter, we discuss three major consequences of the lockdown periods specifically related to the redistribution of time that arise from our data: the pressures and demands of a shift to working at home; the effect of the blurring of work and leisure time; and the effect of reduced commuting hours on reading habits. As Davies et al. (2022, p. 24) identify in their study of lockdown reading

> [...] the pairing of books and the time to read them did not come as easily or as evenly with the Corona-19 lockdowns as one might have hoped. For a high number of people globally, those modern pressures of work simply shifted online in 2020. This entailed many learning new technologies and skillsets in short amounts of time.

This chapter explores how our participants reflected on the relationship between reading and time during the lockdown period. We begin with an overview of research on frequency of reading, and the effect of the lockdown on work and leisure activity. We then turn to our dataset to examine participants' responses drawing on a thematic analysis of free-text responses to one of the questions in our survey and applying both Conceptual Metaphor Theory (Lakoff and Johnson 1980) and the notion of construal (Langacker 2008) to examine how participants talk about reading and time.

2 CONTEXT

2.1 Reading Frequency in Lockdown

Given the constraints of lockdown, which included limited travel and increased working from home, we might well expect an impact on the time participants could spend on reading. On the one hand, given reduced opportunities for social activities, we might imagine that more time was available for reading. On the other hand, a reduction in commuting for some and the increase in home-working and in home-schooling may have impacted on the amount of time previously used for reading.

Studies of reading frequency are not rare. For example, a YouGov poll of just over seven thousand readers taken in March 2020, just before the first lockdown, reported that just over a third of respondents reported reading more than once a week (with a fifth reading every day), although the percentage for those reporting they rarely or never read was similar. Reading frequency increased with age (those in the 55+ category read more), there was a difference in gender (females read more than males), and it seems that there is such a thing as a 'frequent' or 'heavy' reader. Studies such as the YouGov survey (see also similar surveys by The Reading Agency 2017 and Kantar 2021) often present reading frequency as a discriminator within a typology of readerly attributes, and this is a trait that is also identified in studies of young readers (e.g. Hughes-Hassell and Rodge 2007; and see the annual National Literacy Trust reading surveys [National Literacy Trust] 2023). Yu and O'Brien (1999), for example, survey 300 readers across two UK libraries on their reading habits and characterised frequent and non-frequent readers based on the number of books borrowed and reported as read per week. In turn, several studies of the effect of lockdown on reading habits in different countries and with different groups report that reading generally did increase (e.g. Clark and Picton 2020; Navas-Martín et al. 2021; John and Bindiya Tater 2022; The Reading Agency 2022) and vary as readers engaged with texts in different ways (Chalari and Marios Vryonides 2022). There is also some evidence to suggest that an increase in reading activity during lockdown periods had a positive effect on emotional wellbeing (Alomari et al. 2022) and even on attitudes to reading per se (Adeyemi 2021).

2.2 *Caring Responsibilities*

As well as the home morphing into the office space, many people were asked to take on additional caring responsibilities for family members and/or home school their children. In the latter case, significant amounts of time had to be allocated to looking after the education of children (Calear et al. 2022), and this was detrimental to parents' and caregivers' wellbeing (Office for National Statistics 2020). Lockdown periods resulted in the relationship between traditionally separate spheres of work and leisure activity becoming more complex (Sivan 2020). Studies highlight that lockdown periods reduced participation in social activities outside of the home (Lesser and Nienhuis 2020; Liu et al. 2022). Morse et al. (2021) demonstrate that participation in 'creative activities' (such as listening to or playing music, drawing and painting, building, reading, and creative writing) increased during the lockdown months while participation in 'non-creative activities' (such as playing games, socialising, going to the cinema, eating out, playing sports, and travel) decreased. The reduction in these latter activities that typically take place outside the home, together with the added demands of home-working and home-schooling, meant that some people found it more difficult to separate work and leisure time (Marques and Giolo 2020).

2.3 Reading and Commuting

Reading on the commute to work is a very good example of what is known as 'travel-based multitasking', defined as 'the engagement or participation in other activities while simultaneously traveling' (Singleton 2020, p. 150). In other words, as well as spending time travelling, passengers on buses, trains, and trams and non-drivers in cars may be able to expend mental energy on other tasks such as reading, writing, listening to music, and other forms of productive labour[1] since they are not responsible for the mode of transportation itself. The particular mode of transport may be considered active (e.g. driving a car) or passive (e.g. being a passenger on a train); equally, activities may be active (e.g. reading) or passive (e.g. sleeping). The relationship between modes and activities may be straightforward: for example, a passive mode allows any kind of activity, or more complex such as in the case of driving a car; an active mode permits some active activity (the act of driving itself) but not others (e.g. reading) and no passive ones (see Kenyon 2010; Circella et al. 2012; Shaw et al. 2019). Pre-lockdown research on such behaviour has found that there is some variety between the modes; for example, car drivers are most likely to listen to music while train passengers are most likely to undertake active activities such as reading or writing (Russell et al. 2011). Overall, there is evidence to suggest that travel-based multitasking offers commuters the opportunity to make more valuable use of their travelling time should they wish to do so (Molin et al. 2019). Since the lockdowns resulted in a reduction in commuting (Kun et al. 2020; Kogus et al. 2023), we might expect the opportunity to undertake different kinds of multitasking, including reading, to also decrease. Indeed, Nikolaeva et al. (2023) report that during lockdown, passengers report differing levels of missing commuting or 'commute appreciation' (see also Aoustin and Levinson 2021). The interviewees in their study reported mixed feelings about the loss of commute

---

[1] Relaxing is also a form of multi-tasking according to Singleton as is exercise (a byproduct of travelling by bike or running/walking).

with some explicitly mentioning the loss of reading time as negative despite a generally positive feeling about not having to commute.

> I do not like commuting and I welcome the increased time for sleep and relaxation. (...) Part of the reason for this is also that my train commute takes place on a very crowded route and I often have to stand for part of the journey. I do notice that I do not read as much anymore, as I usually do this during my train ride. (Nikolaeva et al. 2023, p. 13)

We now turn to our data to examine these issues in more detail focusing on what our participants said about their perceived sense of time during the lockdown, how changes to their routine impacted on their reading habits, and how they viewed the relationship between reading, time, and mental health.

3   Methodology

The data in this chapter are drawn from Questions 5 and 5a of the *Aston Lockdown Reading Survey Corpus* and are analysed using a combination of approaches and methods. First, the results of responses to Question 5 are simply presented numerically; more extensive data were generated through the free-text responses to Question 5a. These form the basis of longer discussion in Sect. 4.1, which presents our analysis of a sub-corpus comprising all 668 responses to Question 5a, totalling 11,567 tokens. Responses were open coded using NVivo to draw attention to emerging patterns in response using an inductive method. Following a first round of coding, a second round of axial coding refined the original codes to generate a set of themes, and these form the basis for our analysis. In Sects. 4.2 and 4.3, we examine in closer linguistic detail some of the responses related specifically to representations of 'time' and 'reading'. Here, we draw upon methods from corpus linguistics to examine word frequencies, collocates, and concordance lines using *Sketch Engine*.

4   Analysis

The responses to Question 5 ('Since the start of the lockdown, I have been reading...') are displayed in Table 3.1.

Table 3.1 Summary of responses to Question 5

Option	Number and percentage of responses selecting option
About the same as I would normally	195 (22.67%)
Less than I would normally	172 (20%)
More than I would normally	492 (57.21%)
No answer	1 (0.12%)

The figures show that of the participants in our survey, the majority reported reading more. Just over a fifth reported that their reading habits in terms of time spent on reading had not changed since the pandemic began and slightly fewer participants reported that they had been reading less.

4.1 Reasons for Changes in Reading Habits

In the following section, we analyse the free-text responses of those who answered b) or c) to Question 5. Here we examine how participants reported in any changes in the amount of time they spent reading during the early lockdown period.

4.1.1 Changing Relationship with Reading

As demonstrated in Table 3.1, a majority of participants said that they had read more than they normally would pre-lockdown. In many cases, this was reported in a simple way, for example, 'more time to read' (Participant 2) and 'I have more time than before lockdown' (Participant 47). On other occasions, the increase in time aligned with a more intrinsic and personal motivation; for example, Participant 154 noted that 'I made it part of my daily routine to read'. An interesting observation regarding increased reading time and external forms of motivation came from Participant 219, who drew attention to how Amazon's marketing strategy acted as a push to encourage a personal commitment to read more.

> [...] a lot of my favourite authors gave lists of their recommended books during lockdown and they made me curious, so I found a lot of new favourites. And, at the beginning, Amazon cut the prices of a lot of Kindle books which I wanted, so it made me feel like in a competition with myself to do this now, before the world returns to "normal".

4.1.2 Work Patterns and Commuting

In other instances, more specific points regarding the relationship between changing work patterns and increased reading emerge. For example, the shift to working from home as the norm seemed to provide a space for some participants to read more. Participant 223, for example, reported that 'I've read slightly more because working from home I have more time to read'. A number of participants specifically discussed the impact of the loss of their commute and the way that it freed up more time that they had chosen to spend reading. Participant 262 drew specific attention to the loss of a commute which, to them, had led to more time available for and being used to read 'I'm staying up later at night, because I am working from home and don't have to get up early to catch a train'. In some instances, participants reflected not just on the increased reading time but on the perception of their commute. For example, Participant 252 remarked that they saw the commute as 'time wasted travelling to and from university', while Participant 285 commented that 'my day is no longer dominated by commuting or regular work tasks'. In these examples, the two adjectives 'wasted' and 'dominated' provide an interesting insight into how 'commute appreciation'. In another interesting comment, participant 379 highlighted how time had been gained through no longer needing to prepare 'to (sic) travel to work (hair, shoes, packing my bag, etc.)' was able to be used to read. Another participant reflected on the nature of the commute itself which was 'disrupted by changes and walking so I mostly listen to music, podcasts, audible' (487). For these participants, their increased reading time had led them to reflect on the constraints of their pre-lockdown commute. In other instances, participants outlined how a lack of commute resulted in being less tired and more energetic so that they actually felt they could take up reading again. This sense was evident in comments such as 'I think the lack of commuting has made me less tired overall'(Participant 718) and 'Staying at home all day has saved up about 2 hours of commute time to and from university, which also means I am less tired' (729).

Of those participants who reported that reading time had decreased since the start of lockdown, a number commented that this decrease was due to reduced commuting time. Many reflected that their commute had provided most of their weekly reading time often explicitly quantifying that loss, for example:

I've lost my commute (1 h a day reading time). (Participant 121)

Working from home doesn't allow any more time for reading, and loss of commuting time (2 h daily) was a big factor. (Participant 168)

[S]o before lockdown I was reading on a train nearly 4 h per week. (Participant 311)

I used to read a lot on my 45-min train commute each day, and now I just wake up later and work longer hours. (Participant 584)

I used my commute as a quiet time to read for a total of one hour a day (usually a mix of news/entertainment articles online and physical books such as novels and research material). (Participant 224)

In other instances, participants made even more explicit reference to the fact that they had used their commute time strategically. For example, Participant 721 commented on how they 'would normally read around my commute', outlining how the absence of that structured and dedicated time meant they would be 'less likely to carve out specific time to read'. Interestingly, Participant 588 commented that their entire enthusiasm and appetite for reading had decreased as a result of 'No commuting to get me "into" a book that I then want to carry on reading when I get home'. Other participants, however, expressed the opposite sentiment. Participant 355, for example, outlined how they had purposefully 're-instigated a habit' during lockdown, ensuring that they made space to compensate for the reduction of commuting time during which reading had previously taken place.

4.1.3 Social Activities

Comments surrounding the impact of decreased social activities were also prevalent. Participants spoke about the gaps that appeared as a result of not 'eating out' (Participant 11), 'not [being] out at clubs and societies' (Participant 174), not going to the 'theatre, cinema etc.' (Participant 247), 'museums, galleries, parks' (Participant 679) and 'hanging with friends, watching a film, going out for food/clubs' (Participant 299). In other instances, the lack of opportunities to travel imposed by the lockdown conditions were commented on. For example, Participant 107 outlined how 'Easter was very relaxing with no marking and no travel', drawing attention to how the enforced change in behaviour had had a positive effect which had led to an increased desire to read. Participant 787 similarly highlighted the positive impact on reading habits of gained time as a result of not 'travelling long distances to visit my family, as I did before lockdown'. In these examples, participants seemed to value the benefits of reduced travel and social activities; as Participant 674 put it, the lockdown meant that there were fewer 'distractions' which allowed for more reading time. In a different kind of construal, reading was viewed as more of a compensation for the lockdown restrictions on social activity; Participant 185 mentioned that reading replaced 'travel to see friends', and Participant 299 described reading as 'Being in lockdown where we can only stay in doors (sic), reading more has been a great way to pass time and entertain myself'.

4.1.4 Televisions and Screens

Another theme that emerged from our data was that reading became a powerful antidote to watching television and from prolonged exposure to screens as a result of working from home with its increased reliance on video platforms such as Teams and Zoom to conduct meetings. Often, participants spoke about taking up reading as a way of relieving the monotony of television programmes, for example:

> Rediscovered reading after getting bored of binging Netflix. (Participant 859)

> You get bored of TV and want to escape lockdown. (Participant 79)

> I usually read very little but have tried to force myself to be more productive and not just tune into endless hours of Netflix. (Participant 682)

> Eventually I switched off the 24 h news and my reading increased gradually. (Participant 457)

Others spoke of the pull of reading compared to a growing dissatisfaction with television and in particular its reporting of the pandemic. This manifested itself in strong comments such as 'Disgusted with TV and the BBC particularly' (Participant 8), and in comments where reading was construed as a 'welcome distraction from bad news and worrying news [on television] about Covid-19' (Participant 306). As Participant 212 commented, 'I've been avoiding news and television so reading has been a good escape'. The desire to move away from reporting of the pandemic was not confined to television; several participants reported reading more in order to 'take a break from social media' (Participant 399) and as outlined by Participant 833, 'I found myself dipping too much into social media at the onset [...] Redirecting time to reading was much more enjoyable'.

Increased screen time through working commitments at home and remote meetings also appeared to influence social choices around reading. Participant 259 spoke of being 'Exhausted by video conferencing for work', and Participant 331 explicitly identified their increased reading time as a result of 'Actively seeking ways to not look at a screen'. As Participant 185 explained, the almost complete replacement of face to face work and social activity with online, virtual meetings with others made watching television less appealing as a pastime. For this participant, reading offered a calming respite from the computer screen:

> The combination of working from home and using video calls to socialise has meant that I've spent much more time staring at screens. When I have spare time, the idea of staring at another screen to watch TV or a film just hasn't appealed at all—whereas opening a book felt much more relaxing!

4.1.5 Caring Responsibilities

Unsurprisingly, another reason participants gave for a reduction in reading time was increased caring responsibilities. These ranged from caring for elderly, unwell, or vulnerable family members to caring for children whose schools had closed and, with some exceptions such as children of key workers, were homeschooled. With the closure of schools, many participants reported being 'super busy with work and childcare' (Participant 121), playing 'endless board games and videos with kids' (Participant 171), and burdened by the added strain of children 'permanently in the house and not out at clubs and societies' (Participant 174). As Participant 6 put it, 'A lot of it is trying to set a better example to my kids, who are home all the time now'. Home-schooling was also mentioned by many participants, often identifying the demands of 'juggling working from home with supporting my children learning at home' (Participant 472), where 'My workload has increased plus trying to combine full time work and home schooling' (Participant 745). As Participant 415 stated, '[I] am temporarily a busy teaching assistant'. In some cases, however, participants reported that the closure of schools led to a reduction in travel and, subsequently, to more time being available. Participant 269 explained that 'this means some of my early mornings can be spent reading', and Participant 511 reported that they were 'Spending less time ferrying children about so had more time'. Some parents were able to use time when supervising their children's work to read, for example, Participant 269 who wrote, 'I can't do other work further away from her in case she needs help.' A further observation from some participants was that reading increased as a result of home schooling as a practice which gave back some personal time that had been used working with children. As Participant 182 wrote, 'Reading has been an escape from work, homeschooling and any anxieties around the pandemic'. Equally, Participant 641 wrote that 'After spending all day homeschooling 2 kids, reading is a way of escaping and taking time for me'. Surprisingly, very few of our participants reported reading more to their children.

4.1.6   Access to Books

Some readers did explicitly mention access in relation to perceived changes in quantity of their reading. Participant 639 commented that they had 'Joined "The pigeonhole" app just as lockdown was happening, access to more books, so reading more'; equally, Participant 751 highlighted how

> I started reading less because I had no access to books I hadn't read before. Then I found the Libby app[2] where I can get library books on my tablet so I've been churning through quite a few.

Indeed it appears that reading apps and forms of e-reading mitigated the effect the lockdown period had had on other ways of accessing books. Several participants, for example, outlined how the closure of public libraries meant that they had significantly less access to books.

4.1.7   Mental Health

Mental health was a significant theme in participants' responses. Many spoke of how their general anxiety and lack of focus had affected the quantity of reading since the start of lockdown. Indeed, the various forms of 'concentrate' ('concentrate', 'concentrates', 'concentration' and so on) appear 54 times in the Question 5a sub-corpus. Participants specifically commented on having 'Difficulty concentrating' (Participant 132), being 'Unable to focus' (Participant 148), and having 'more distractions' (Participant 169). Some participants outlined how the lockdown had affected their ability to engage with books; drawing on the common READING IS TRANSPORTATION and READING IS IMMERSION[3] metaphors (see Gerrig 1993; Stockwell 2020; and further discussion in Chap. 5), they reported experiences such as:

---

[2] The Pigeonhole and Libby apps allow readers to borrow e-books. Marketed as 'the book club in your pocket', The Pigeonhole also enables readers to discuss their reading with others.
[3] We follow the standard convention which is to present metaphors in small capitals.

> Reading doesn't feel like as much *of an escape*, because now it's [the lockdown] all the time, every day. (Participant 179)
>
> Difficulty concentrating and inability *to sink* into the story. (Participant 214)
>
> I have found it hard to concentrate and *immerse* myself in stories as much as I normally would. (Participant 240)
>
> [C]ouldn't *get into* anything that I was reading, even authors that I normally enjoy. (Participant 815)
>
> [I have] apprehension about *emotional engagement* with the unknown (ie new books). (Participant 255)

Participants also recognised that their anxiety resulted in 'focusing attention elsewhere' (Participant 249). Participant 268, for example, identified how pre-lockdown reading time had been replaced by watching the news. This seemed particularly prevalent in the early stages of lockdown and a number of participants made a distinction between the first few weeks of lockdown and shifting behaviours a little later. As Participant 654 wrote:

> At the beginning of lockdown I couldn't read much at all—my concentration was shot. Gradually though the Covid fear started to subside into Covid anxiety and reading became escapism.

Interestingly, this initial period of reading inertia was typically quantified as between 3 and 6 weeks; Participant 483's response below is typical of a number of reports of the impact of the first weeks of the lockdown.

> I found it hard to concentrate on reading for the first six weeks or so and read much less than normal.

There were participants, however, who reported that the positive mental health benefits of reading had increased the amount of time spent with books. Many said that they had been reading more because they recognised and felt the therapeutic benefits of reading. They used phrases such as 'A way to manage stress and anxiety' (Participant 133), 'Allowing myself to relax a little' (Participant 138), 'Desire to enrich my mind' (Participant 139), and 'to keep my mind alert' (Participant 144). Many also drew on the same READING IS TRANSPORTATION and READING IS IMMERSION metaphors that those who reported reading less used. Here, words such as 'escape' and 'distraction' were used as an explanation of and justification for more reading (our added emphases):

Reading has been *an escape* from work, homeschooling and any anxieties around the pandemic. (Participant 182)

I have also taken the opportunity *to escape* the real world. (Participant 190)

To escape the misery of real life and seek comfort and relief in imaginative worlds. (Participant 202)

More free time to read, chance *to escape* the misery of 2020. (Participant 207)

I'm aiming to keep up as many habits and hobbies as possible *to distract* from the drudgery of life in lockdown. (Participant 226)

I have found books *a welcome distraction* from bad news and the worrying news about Covid-19. (Participant 306)

More time plus enjoy *the diversion*. (Participant 421)

In other instances, participants articulated that they were reading more because it provided them with some kind of structure to the day, as highlighted here by Participant 816, 'Reading gave me a good daily structure during lockdown and became part of my evening wind-down before bed'. And participants reported that they felt the stress-relieving properties of reading, from being, as Participant 757 put it, 'trapped in the house'. One further interesting construal was used by Participant 601 who wrote that 'Reading is also like a "paralysing" agent. It alleviates my stress'. Here reading is perceived as acting directly on the reader, a representation of reading that we examine in more detail in Sect. 4.3.

4.2 The Perception of Time

As we discussed in the previous section, participants made extensive reference to the concept of time when discussing their reading. In this section, we extend the discussion by exploring how time appears in the sub-corpus of responses to Question 5a, and specifically as related to the use of particular metaphors to frame their understanding of time related to the quality and quantity of their reading.

As Table 3.2 demonstrates, 'time' is the most frequently occurring noun lemma in the Question 5a sub-corpus (n = 425), occurring more times than the total sum of the nouns in positions 2–6.

We can build on this observation by undertaking a collocation analysis, which generates information on how a particular word is used in context.

Table 3.2 Frequency rank of the ten most frequently occurring noun lemmas in the Question 5a sub-corpus

Rank	Noun lemma	Frequency	% of all noun lemmas
1	Time	425	17.71
2	Book	103	4.29
3	Home	103	4.29
4	Reading	83	3.46
5	Lockdown	70	2.92
6	Work	64	2.67
7	Lot	43	1.79
8	Day	39	1.63
9	Commute	33	1.38
10	Evening	29	1.21

Collocation analysis typically measures 'the association between words based on patterns of co-occurrence' (Brookes, 2023, p. 218). In this instance, collocates of the node word 'time' are examined to explore more precisely the ways in which 'time' is conceived of and utilised by the participants in our study. Using Sketch Engine's *Word Sketch* feature, we do this first by focusing on modifiers of time, and then verb collocates of time occurring in subject and object positions. Table 3.3 shows the top ten modifiers of 'time' in our sub-corpus. These are ranked by their LogDice score (Rychlý 2008), which is an association measure that favours 'collocates which occur exclusively in each other's company but do not have to be rare' (Brezina, 2018, p. 70), thus indicating how strong the collocation is.

The collocation analysis demonstrates that, in our sub-corpus, time is viewed as quantifiable and gradable ('more', 'less' 'extra'), is presented as something that can be possessed by an owner, and is a resource that can be used as the owner sees fit. For example, 'I have the spare time to read' positions the participant as in control of a particular type of capital that can be utilised as desired. The representation of time as a phenomenon to be owned and controlled extends into personal constructs of time in noun phrases such as '*my quiet* time' and those occasions where 'time' is modified by another noun, for example, '*commute* time', '*leisure* time', and '*reading* time'. In these latter two instances, participants compartmentalise time into particular strands of use or as a resource for a specific purpose. The data from our sub-corpus therefore show that participants draw on what are well-established metaphors in western culture by which a concept idea (time) is given structured and understood through reference to a more concrete entity. According to Lakoff and Johnson (1980,

Table 3.3 Top modifiers of 'time' in the Question 5a sub-corpus

Rank	Collocate	Co-occurrences	LogDice score	Example
1	Free	53	12.46	More *free time* and a need to use the extra time wisely
2	More	112	12.45	I had *more time* on my hands as I wasn't at work every single day as normal
3	Lot	12	10.54	I had a *lot* more *time* on weekends I couldn't do other hobbies
4	Spare	8	10.04	An increased sense that I have the *spare time* to read
5	Less	10	9.96	Spending *less time* seeing friends, so needing to fill the evenings
6	Extra	5	9.35	I have two days when I have been furloughed from work, which gives me a little *extra time*
7	Commute	3	8.64	Staying at home all day has saved up about 2 hours of *commute time*
8	Leisure	3	8.6	Sunnier weather to enjoy reading in garden more *leisure time*. More socially acceptable to not be as productive as usual
9	Reading	4	8.46	However, I've lost some *reading time* in that I'm no longer commuting by train
10	Quiet	2	8.06	I've lost my 2-hour daily round-trip commute, which used to be my *quiet time*

pp. 80–89), metaphors of time such as TIME IS MONEY, TIME IS A RESOURCE, and TIME IS A COMMODITY draw on industrialised processes in which 'We understand and experience time as the kind of thing that can be spent, wasted, budgeted, invested wisely or poorly, saved or squandered'.

It seems then, then aside of some local instances where collocates of 'time' perhaps appear more specifically linked to the events of lockdown ('commute' and 'leisure'), participants tend to fall back on more conventional metaphors for time. Given that more generally the pandemic gave rise to several new metaphors as people came to terms with rapidly changing times (see, e.g. Semino 2021; Döring and Nerlich 2022), this conservatism might seem unusual. In order to explore this more, we can look at the instances where time is used as an object and examine its verb collocates. Table 3.4 shows the top verb collocates with 'time' as their object in our sub-corpus. Again, these are ranked by their LogDice score.

Table 3.4 Top verb collocates with 'time' as their object

Rank	Collocate	Co-occurrences	LogDice score	Example
1	Have	83	12.1	Because I *have* more *time* to read.
2	Spend	22	11.73	I have not *spent time* travelling long distances to visit my family, as I did before lockdown
3	Fill	4	9.68	Because I read and watch shows to *fill* the *time*
4	Take	3	8.89	Reading is a way of escaping and *taking time* for me
5	Get	3	8.82	I've *got* more *time*
6	Manage	2	8.74	Struggled to *manage time* and energy in the evening
7	Find	3	8.68	I have *found time* to read more in the evenings instead of doing other things
8	Lose	2	8.62	However, I've *lost* some reading *time* in that I'm no longer commuting by train
9	Leave	2	8.62	Spending much less time on social activities, *leaving* more *time* for reading
10	Use	2	8.32	I have *used* this *time* to read more

The collocates listed in Table 3.4 again confirm that the predominance of the metaphors TIME IS MONEY, TIME IS A RESOURCE, and TIME IS A COMMODITY realised in verbs which highlights various ways in which time can be acquired, owned, controlled, and utilised. One further interesting representation draws specifically on a CONTAINER schema (Johnson 1987) to objectify time as a physical space that can be filled with something; in the example concordance, time is 'filled' by reading and television. In this construal, time is conceived as an overarching frame or space, rendered available due to the specific constraints of the lockdown period (lack of work, lack of social commitments, and so on).

4.3 Reading As an Agentive Figure

In this next section, we examine the ways in which participants represent the act of reading. The word *reading* occurs 150 times in the responses to Question 5a, most frequently in its present participle form 'reading', forming a verb phrase with a form of the copular auxiliary 'to be', for example, 'I was reading', 'I am reading'. Here, however, we look at those instances where it is construed a noun and assigned the subject role functioning as an agent in the clause (n = 41). In doing so, we draw on the theory of Cognitive Grammar (CG) and Langacker's *event participant roles* (Langacker 2008), which provide a template for examining the various semantic roles inherent in clause structures. Langacker's model is built around the notion of a prototypical clause on which subject (an agent) acts on another (a patient) to cause some change in state. Typically, in this configuration, the agent acts as the primary participant in an action chain and the 'energy source' (Langacker 2008, p. 356), whilst the patient, affected by the action of the agent, is the endpoint in the chain or 'energy sink'. Overall, various kinds of syntactic representation are covered by CG's notion of 'construal' which draws attention to how a scene might be represented (construed) in different ways, each of which imports some meaning.

In their study of metaphors for reading in online responses to the *Twilight* series of books, Nuttall and Harrison (2020) highlight how readers tend to frame the relationship between reader and text using one of two types of participant role. In the first, the reader is construed as an agent acting on the text (patient), for example, where a reader talks of '*getting into*' a book. The second is the inverse relationship where text is the agent acting on the reader (patient) who is consequently altered in some way by the experience, for example, 'I *was pulled into* this love story'. In our data, participants appear to offer a slightly different construal when using nominalising *reading*, presenting the act itself (rather than the reader or the text) more clearly as a clausal subject engaging as an agent or some other kind of intermediary role, as we discuss below.

Table 3.5 shows a sample set of concordance lines for *reading*; lines 1–6 are examples of instances (27 out of 41 in total) where reading is positioned as the clausal subject in processes that denote states of being (e.g. using the verb phrases 'has become' or 'has been'). In these instances, *reading* is construed as an instrument (Langacker 2008, p. 356), an intermediary phenomenon, rather than a source of energy in its own right, which enables the participant to achieve something, in these instances, 'a good escape', 'a way of distancing myself', 'a wonderful way to fill the time', and so on. Overall, these construals might be summarised using an overarching metaphor of READING IS (EMOTIONAL) SUPPORT, explicitly marked in the first example, 'reading has become a crutch'. Here, reading is thus framed as a mental analogue of the physical crutch, which helps support the reader by keeping them upright and steady. In turn, then, this

Table 3.5 Sample concordance lines for *reading*

1	Given the current situation	Reading	has become a crutch
2	Work	Reading	has become all online
3	I've been avoiding news and television so	Reading	has been a good escape
4	I also think	Reading	has been a way of distancing myself
5	As I am widowed and live alone	Reading	has been a wonderful way to fill months of isolation
6		Reading	has been an escape from work
7	It's been a very uncertain period of time and	Reading	has brought me helpful solace
8	I have been home schooling and	Reading	has given me a much needed escape
9	I am not mentally stimulated at work so	Reading	has helped keep my brain active
10		Reading	has offered a private escape from the world
11	I've been anxious about the pandemic and	Reading	helps my anxiety

construal also draws on a more conventional orientational metaphor GOOD IS UP (see Lakoff and Johnson 1980, pp. 14–21), by which physical and mental health is conceived as upright direction and/or movement (compare, e.g., a phrase such as 'I'm down').

Examples 7–11 also offer interesting construals as participants frame *reading* across specific participant roles. In examples 7 and 8, ditransitive structures, including both indirect and direct objects after the verb phrase, are used to highlight how reading brings some aspect (usually positive) to the recipient (participant). These structures again move beyond the archetypal action chain that we introduced earlier since although they present *reading* as an agentive force, they do so by combining the role of agent with thematic (Langacker 2008, p. 370) roles, in which an energy source is omitted or implied but not directly stated. One such participant role is a 'mover', which undergoes a change of location through time, either of its own accord or as an integral part of the verb used. In ditransitive structures, CG treats indirect objects (e.g. following verbs such as 'to give' and 'to bring') as an 'experiencers', the recipient(s) of the verbal action. The clause structure in examples 7 and 8 is thus tripartite, and each participant is profiled (given attention) through the construal:

Reading (AGENT) has brought me (EXPERIENCER) helpful solace (MOVER)

Reading (AGENT) has given me (EXPERIENCER) a much needed escape (MOVER)

In the final examples, the agentive nature of *reading* is similarly highlighted, drawing attention to how it is a force that allows the recipient to experience the world in some way. In examples 9–11, participants' choices of verbs, 'helped', 'offered', 'helps' more explicitly draw attention to the agent-recipient relationship and suggest another interesting metaphorical construal, READING IS A CAREGIVER. We see this metaphor realised in the roles assigned to participants in each of the clauses and in the specific lexical choices contained within those roles; for example, a pattern that seems to emerge is the 'mover' role being filled by noun phrase with a single pre-modifier (*'helpful* solace', *'much needed* escape').

Overall, the analysis of construals of *reading* used by participants in the sub-corpus of responses to Question 5a highlights the agency assigned by participants in a way that focuses not on a process concerned with the interactional relationship between a reader and a text but on the reification of that process as a perceived agentive entity in its own right. In other words, participants speak of reading as though it is a co-participant in a process rather than the process itself and foreground the consequences and effects of its actions in ways which draw attention to themselves as experiencers and recipients of actions perceived as under the control of *reading*.

5   Conclusion

The analysis of our data in this chapter identifies that reading habits did change in terms of frequency of reading during those first lockdown months and that in our study, people were generally reading more. The data demonstrate that there seemed to be internal and external motivators for a change in reading frequency. First, the external context in the form of working from home and reductions in travel and in leisure activities provided participants with extra time. In this way, time now became a resource that could be used, spent, or filled by reading. Alternatively there were internal motivators such as the need to find some sense of structure in the midst of radical upheaval, a desire to relieve stress or simply the wish to indulge in a pleasurable activity. In this way, reading itself was foregrounded as central to lockdown experiences.

Our data also identify particular ways in which time was represented or construed. The metaphors used by our participants highlighted how participants reflected on time and its relationship to them. Given that our survey was completed during the first few months of the UK lockdown period, it is perhaps unsurprising that participants drew on very common ways of conceiving time. It was, however, interesting to see the ways in which reading was similarly construed. One interesting construal that we have discussed in this chapter is the metaphor READING IS A CAREGIVER. It seems that for some participants, reading did appear to provide some kind of therapeutic benefit (see further discussion in Chap. 5), and they consequently presented reading as an agentive figure with some degree of influence over them. Since generally participants who drew on this particular metaphor reported their experience of lockdown being positive or at least improving as the weeks and months passed, we might assume that this specific construal is a helpful one and might have potential to be used in other bibliotherapeutic contexts as a way of providing support through trauma.[4]

This latter example highlights a key finding from our data: that reasons for changes in reading frequency were often connected to mental health issues. Indeed, while reading was cited as an activity that mitigated concerns and worries about the virus, it was also the case that pre-lockdown regular readers reported that the frequency of their reading had been affected by a lack of concentration and inability to engage with books that the lockdown had brought. Some of these concerns were, of course, heightened by the demands that some participants faced in terms of working from home and caring responsibilities.

REFERENCES

Adeyemi, Ismail Olatunji. 2021. Influence of COVID-19 lockdown on reading habit of Nigerians: A case study of Lagos state inhabitants. *Reading & Writing Quarterly* 37 (2): 157–168. https://doi.org/10.1080/10573569.2020.1857891.

Alomari, Mahmoud A., Karem H. Alzoubi, Omar F. Khabour, and Manal Hendawi. 2022. Negative emotional symptoms during COVID19 confinement: The relationship with reading habits. *Informatics in Medicine Unlocked* 31: 100962. https://doi.org/10.1016/j.imu.2022.100962.

---

[4] Of course READING IS A CAREGIVER may not be a positive metaphor for everyone.

Aoustin, Louise, and David M. Levinson. 2021. Longing to travel: Commute appreciation during COVID-19. *Findings* 18523. https://doi.org/10.32866/001c.18523.

Brezina, V. 2018. *Statistics in corpus linguistics: A practical guide.* Cambridge: Cambridge University Press.

Brookes, Gavin. 2023. Killer, thief or companion? A corpus-based study of dementia metaphors in UK tabloids. *Metaphor and Symbol* 38 (3): 213–230. https://doi.org/10.1080/10926488.2022.2142472.

Calear, Alison L., Sonia McCallum, Alyssa R. Morse, Michelle Banfield, Amelia Gulliver, Nicolas Cherbuin, Louise M. Farrer, Kristen Murray, Rachael M. Rodney Harris, and Philip J. Batterham. 2022. Psychosocial impacts of home-schooling on parents and caregivers during the COVID-19 pandemic. *BMC Public Health* 22: 119. https://doi.org/10.1186/s12889-022-12532-2.

Chalari, Maria, and M. Marios Vryonides. 2022. Adolescents' reading habits during COVID-19 protracted lockdown: To what extent do they still contribute to the perpetuation of cultural reproduction? *International Journal of Educational Research* 115. https://doi.org/10.1016/j.ijer.2022.102012.

Circella, Giovanna, Patricia L. Mokhtarian, and Laura K. Poff. 2012. A conceptual typology of multitasking behavior and polychronicity preferences. *Electronic International Journal of Time Use Research* 9 (1): 59–107.

Clark, Christina, and Irene Picton. 2020. "It makes me feel like I'm in a different place, not stuck inside." children and young people's reading in 2020 before and during the COVID-19 lockdown. *National Literacy Trust Research Report.*

Davies, Ben, Christina Lupton, and Johanne Gormsen Schmidt. 2022. *Reading novels during the Covid-19 pandemic.* Oxford: Oxford University Press.

Döring, Martin, and Brigitte Nerlich. 2022. Introduction to special issue. Framing the 2020 coronavirus pandemic: Metaphors, images and symbols. *Metaphor and Symbol* 37 (2): 71–75. https://doi.org/10.1080/10926488.2021.2004378.

Gerrig, Richard J. 1993. *Experiencing narrative worlds: On the psychological activities of reading.* New Haven: Yale University Press.

Hughes-Hassell, Sandra, and Pradnya Rodge. 2007. The leisure reading habits of urban adolescents. *Journal of Adolescent & Adult Literacy* 51 (1): 22–33.

John, Kishor, and B. Bindiya Tater. 2022. Changing reading habits of faculty of higher education in India: A study of the COVID-19 lockdown period. *The Serials Librarian* 83 (1): 60–80.

Johnson, Mark. 1987. *The body in the mind.* Chicago: Chicago University Press.

Kantar. 2021. 'Are people still reading physical books?', https://www.kantar.com/uki/inspiration/sport-leisure/are-people-still-reading-physical-books.

Kenyon, Susan. 2010. What do we mean by multitasking?–exploring the need for methodological clarification in time use research. *Electronic International Journal of Time Use Research* 7 (1): 42–60.

Kilgarriff, Adam, Vít Baisa, Jan Bušta, Miloš Jakubíček, Vojtěch Kovář, Jan Michelfeit, Pavel Rychlý, and Vít Suchomel. 2014. The sketch engine: Ten years on. *Lexicography* 1 (7–36): 2014. https://www.sketchengine.eu/wp-content/uploads/The_Sketch_Engine_2014.pdf.

Kogus, Ayelet, Ayelet Gal-Tzur, and Yoram Shiftan. 2023. Modelling the long-term expected impact of the covid-19 crisis on commute and telecommute. *Transportation Research Record*: 03611981231160170.

Kun, Andrew, Raffaella Sadun, Orit Shaer, and Thomaz Teodorovicz. 2020. Where did the commute time go? *Harvard Business Review*. https://hbr.org/2020/12/where-did-the-commute-time-go.

Lakoff, George, and Mark Johnson. 1980. *Metaphors we live by*. Chicago: Chicago University Press.

Langacker, Ronald. 2008. *Cognitive grammar: A basic introduction*. New York: Oxford University Press.

Lesser, Iris A., and Carl P. Nienhuis. 2020. The impact of COVID-19 on physical activity behavior and well-being of Canadians. *International Journal of Environmental Research and Public Health* 17 (11): 3899.

Liu, Hung-Ling, Erin S. Lavender-Stott, Christin L. Carotta, and Aileen S. Garcia. 2022. Leisure experience and participation and its contribution to stress-related growth amid COVID-19 pandemic. *Leisure Studies* 41 (1): 70–84. https://doi.org/10.1080/02614367.2021.1942526.

Marques, Lénia, and Guilherme Giolo. 2020. Cultural leisure in the time of COVID-19: Impressions from The Netherlands. *World Leisure Journal* 62 (4): 344–348. https://doi.org/10.1080/16078055.2020.1825256.

Molin, Eric, Kingsley Adjenughwureb, Menno de Bruync, Oded Catsd, and Pim Warffemiuse. 2019. Does conducting activities while traveling reduce the value of evidence from a within-subjects choice experiment. *Transportation Research Part A* 132: 18–29.

Morse, K.F., A. Fine Philip, and Kathryn J. Friedlander. 2021. Creativity and leisure during COVID-19: Examining the relationship between leisure activities, motivations, and psychological well-being. *Frontiers in Psychology* 12: 609967. https://doi.org/10.3389/fpsyg.2021.609967.

National Literacy Trust. 2023. Annual literacy survey, https://literacytrust.org.uk/research-services/annual-literacy-survey/.

Navas-Martín, Miguel Ángel, José Antonio López-Bueno, Ignacio Oteiza, and Teresa Cuerdo-Vilches. 2021. Routines, time dedication and habit changes in Spanish homes during the COVID-19 lockdown. A large cross-sectional survey. *International Journal of Environmental Research and Public Health* 18 (22): 12176. https://doi.org/10.3390/ijerph182212176.

Nikolaeva, Anna, Ying-Tzu Lin, Samuel Nello-Deakin, Ori Rubin, and Kim Carlotta von Schönfeld. 2023. Living without commuting: Experiences of a less mobile life under COVID-19. *Mobilities* 18 (1): 1–20. https://doi.org/10.1080/17450101.2022.2072231.

Nuttall, Louise, and Chloe Harrison. 2020. Wolfing down the twilight series: Metaphors for reading in online reviews. In *Contemporary media stylistics*, ed. Stephen Pihlaja and Helen Ringrow, 35–60. London: Bloomsbury.

Office for National Statistics. 2020. Coronavirus and homeschooling in Great Britain: April to June 2020: Analysis of homeschooling in Great Britain during the coronavirus (COVID-19) pandemic from the Opinions and Lifestyle Survey, https://www.ons.gov.uk/peoplepopulationandcommunity/educationandchildcare/articles/coronavirusandhomeschoolingingreatbritain/apriltojune2020.

Russell, Marie, Rachel Price, Louise Signal, James Stanley, Zachery Gerring, and Jacqueline Cumming. 2011. What do passengers do during travel time? Structured observations on buses and trains. *Journal of Public Transportation* 14 (3): 123–146. https://doi.org/10.5038/2375-0901.14.3.7.

Rychlý, Pavel. 2008. A Lexicographer-Friendly Association Score. Proc. 2nd Workshop on Recent Advances in Slavonic Natural Languages Processing, RASLAN, 2: 6–9. https://www.sketchengine.eu/wp-content/uploads/2015/03/Lexicographer-Friendly_2008.pdf

Semino, Elena. 2021. Not soldiers but fire-fighters - metaphors and covid-19. *Health Communication* 36 (1): 50–58. https://doi.org/10.1080/10410236.2020.1844989.

Shaw, F. Atiyya, Aliaksandr Malokin, Patricia L. Mokhtarian, and Giovanni Circella. 2019. It's not all fun and games: An investigation of the reported benefits and disadvantages of conducting activities while commuting. *Travel Behaviour and Society* 17: 8–25.

Singleton, Patrick A. 2020. Multimodal travel-based multitasking during the commute: Who does what? *International Journal of Sustainable Transportation* 14 (2): 150–162. https://doi.org/10.1080/15568318.2018.1536237.

Sivan, Atara. 2020. Reflection on leisure during COVID-19. *World Leisure Journal* 62 (4): 296–299.

Stockwell, Peter. 2020. *Cognitive poetics: An introduction*. 2nd ed. London: Routledge.

The Reading Agency. 2017. Talking fiction? Research reveals our reading habits and hang-ups', https://readingagency.org.uk/news/media/talking-fiction-research-reveals-nations-reading-habits-and-hang-ups.html.

———. 2022. A quarter of UK adults started reading more during lockdowns and have continued to, finds new survey to mark World Book Night 2022, https://readingagency.org.uk/news/media/a-quarter-of-uk-adults-started-reading-more-during-lockdowns-and-have-continued-to-finds-new-survey.html

Yu, Lianghzi, and Ann O'Brien. 1999. A practical typology of adult fiction borrowers based on their reading habits. *Journal of Information Science* 25 (1): 35–49.

CHAPTER 4

Reading as a Coping Strategy

Abstract This chapter focuses on reading as a coping strategy. We first draw on the relationship between reading and wellbeing and examine some of the ways that reading has been known to have therapeutic value. We then examine how participants reported their use of reading as a positive coping strategy, analysing the reasons they provided for why they turned to reading and drawing attention to the ways in which they framed their experiences. The final part of this chapter discusses findings more broadly to suggest how our data build on and extend what we know about how reading might be used as a coping strategy during times of crisis.

Keywords Reading • Wellbeing • Coping strategies • Public health

1 INTRODUCTION

This chapter builds on our discussion in Chap. 3 by focusing on the role that reading appeared to play in helping participants to cope in a time of crisis. We first draw on the relationship between reading and wellbeing—surveying literature from the health humanities—and examine some of the ways that reading has been known to have therapeutic value, discussing existing research on the therapeutic benefits of reading as a coping

© The Author(s), under exclusive license to Springer Nature
Switzerland AG 2024
A. Boucher et al., *Reading Habits in the COVID-19 Pandemic*,
https://doi.org/10.1007/978-3-031-52753-1_4

strategy. We then discuss our approach to accessing participants' reflections on this topic, which made use of keyness analysis, an inductive method, developed for corpus-assisted discourse studies (CADS), that facilitates the identification of salient topics. Through comparison to a very large reference corpus of internet texts, we identify the top 100 keywords in a 90,000-word sub-corpus of the *Aston Lockdown Reading Survey Corpus* containing all responses to all open questions in the survey. This chapter uses corpus techniques to explore how keywords relating to emergent topics, including comfort, security, escapism, and distraction, provide an insight into participants' reported uses of reading to help them cope during the pandemic.

2 Context

2.1 Reading and Wellbeing

Studies in bibliotherapy (the use of reading to manage physical and mental health challenges) have highlighted the specific ways in which reading literature may promote personal wellbeing (Bate and Schuman 2016; Brewster 2016; McNichol and Brewster 2018) and, more generally, function as a way of coping with life stresses (Gellatly et al. 2007; Gray et al. 2015). In turn, there is a significant body of research that extends the benefits of reading to an increased capacity to understand the mental functioning of others (Oatley 1994; Mar et al. 2006; Kidd and Castano 2013, 2017). Oatley (2016), for example, argues that reading is a kind of simulation in which readers encounter characters and experiences that they might not normally come across in their everyday lives. Active engagement in fictional worlds through recreational reading may bring about both self-change and an awareness of the mental functioning of others, helping individuals process trauma (Green 2020), widen mental capacity (Green 2020), align with others' points of view and promote pro-social behaviour, tolerance of others, and reduce prejudice (Johnson 2012; Lee et al. 2014), and decrease distress and loneliness (Levine et al. 2020). As Green (2020, p. 186) remarks:

> [L]iterature can and does play an analogous and therefore therapeutic role of oblique recognition, standing before the reader in a way that is related in its own medium to how an imaginative doctor stands before a needy patient.

There are some specific studies examining reading as a coping and wellbeing strategy during COVID-19. For example, Waller and Dashwood (2022) highlight how reading and discussing Young Adult fiction in peer groups help teenagers come to terms with the rapid changes and uncertainties brought on by the pandemic. In their survey of children's reading during the pandemic, Topping and Clark (2021) provide data to demonstrate that levels of reading improved during the lockdowns and that reading was often used as a coping strategy to mitigate isolation from friends and family. Equally, in terms of adult readers, Wilkinson (2020) reports on a Scottish Book Trust study which found that reading helped with 'isolation, stress and anxiety [...] to find a sense of normality'. There is also evidence to show that the shifting nature of lockdown reading resulted in new specific motivations for readers: 'reading through fear, reading as escapism and reading about helping' (Kate Nash Literary Agency 2020). And, a quick Google search also reveal a significant number of websites and articles promoting reading and particular books as a coping mechanism to counter the effects of the COVID-19 lockdowns and to increase wellbeing.

While there are other multiple examples of reading being applied to therapeutic contexts directly,[1] including clinical ones, for the purpose of our conception of 'therapy' as it relates to individuals turning autonomously to reading as a means of coping in a time of societal crisis as opposed to personal crisis, we adopt Green's (2020, p. 130) looser notion of 'implicit therapy':

[It] is a specifically Wordsworthian conception of 'therapy' that is being considered here; an oblique process that acts almost by stealth to meet needs that may not even be known consciously to exist.[2]

2.2 Reading as Transportation

Of particular relevance to the context of reading to cope in time of crisis is that reading fiction has been shown to facilitate an emotional 'escape', aiding emotional regulation during times of crisis. Research on how

---

[1] See, for example, the collection of chapters in McNichol and Brewster (2018), which provide a historical overview of bibliotherapy and a range of case studies highlighting how reading has therapeutic value in different contexts.
[2] See also Orr (2002) for a compelling account of reading and writing poetry as a 'survival' mechanism to trauma.

readers conceptualise the reading experience has highlighted the metaphor of transportation, whereby 'a narrative serves to transport an experiencer away from the here and now' (Gerrig 1993, p. 3) and 'returns to the world of origin, somewhat changed by the journey' (Gerrig 1993, p. 11). Through transportation, fictional narratives enable individuals to immerse themselves in different narrative worlds, characters, and scenarios, temporarily diverting their focus from real-life worries. Transportation Theory thus describes 'a convergent process, where all mental systems and capacities become focused on events occurring in the narrative' (Green and Brock 2000, p. 701), therefore resulting in focussed attention and 'loss of access to real-world information' (2000, p. 703). We highlighted this particular metaphor and its realisations in Chap. 3.

Transportation, as facilitated through reading, necessitates focus and attention. Reading poetry, for example, has been shown to be associated with 'greater levels of emotional focus, attentiveness and imagination' when compared to reading non-fiction texts (Green 2020: p. 125). Drawing on the Theory of Mind, attentive engagement with narratives has been shown to draw cognitive processes away from existing preoccupations, activating 'a close link between affective and cognitive components for mentalizing', that is, occupying the brain with the informational and emotional processing required to read the story (Altmann et al. 2012, p. 5). The transportative functions of reading can lead to reduced stress and increased relaxation; the act of reading can thus serve as a mindfulness practice (Dewan 2022), enabling individuals to temporarily disconnect from distressing thoughts and immerse themselves in a narrative that captures their attention.

We now turn to our data to examine what our participants said about the perceived transportive nature of reading during lockdown and its therapeutic uses. Our analyses highlight how our participants viewed reading as a strategy to help them cope with the emotional challenges associated with the lockdown period and the COVID-19 pandemic.

3 Methodology

We analysed a sub-corpus of the *Aston Lockdown Reading Survey Corpus* comprising all responses to the 31 open questions in the survey. As we described in Chap. 1, the sub-corpus contains 6930 individual free-text responses to the open questions and runs to 86,699 tokens. Over 80% of the material in the open question sub-corpus comprises responses to just ten questions (see Appendix 1), which relate to key themes discussed in other chapters of this book, including genre preferences (see Chap. 2), time spent reading (see Chap. 3) and re-reading (see Chap. 5).

Unlike these themes, the theme of reading as a coping strategy was not elicited by the question prompts—i.e., we did not ask participants directly about how they used reading as a coping strategy during the pandemic, and the wordforms *cope* and *coping* appear in the free-text responses only six times. Logically, our approach in this chapter therefore differs to those of the other chapters in this book, which are broadly deductive (or 'top-down') in nature (cf. McEnery and Brezina 2022, p. 17) in that they explore how participants responded to questions addressing specific, pre-determined topics that are imposed upon the data. For instance, in Chap. 3, we explored the use of *time* in a sub-corpus of free-text responses to Question 5a, which elicits responses about how much time was spent reading during the lockdown. In this case, our interest in *time* was therefore determined before the data were collected, so our analysis of *time* adopted what is known as a *corpus-based* approach, which 'avails itself of the corpus mainly to expound, test or exemplify theories and descriptions' (Tognini-Bonelli 2001, p. 65) that were determined before the analysis commenced; we identified a linguistic feature relating to a pre-existing hypothesis and searched for that feature in the data (Mackiewicz and Thompson 2016, p. 190).

In contrast, our approach in this chapter uses inductive (or 'bottom-up') reasoning (cf. McEnery and Brezina 2022, p. 17) by adopting a *corpus-driven* approach, which relies on 'the integrity of the data as a whole' (Tognini-Bonelli 2001, p. 84) to allow features of interest to our research question to emerge from the data through exploration. There are no 'predetermined words'; rather, 'theory...does not exist before the corpus-driven analysis but is developed from it' (Mackiewicz and Thompson 2016, p. 190). In our case, we employed keyness analysis to automatically extract terms (known as *keywords* or *key items*; see e.g. Gabrielatos 2018) that are relatively frequent across the open question responses compared to a reference corpus. Keyness analysis is among the most widely used approaches in corpus-assisted discourse studies (CADS; Partington et al. 2013), allowing for the quantitative identification of 'salient features' (Mackiewicz and Thompson 2016, p. 190) that act as 'signposts' to potentially interesting themes that may be explored qualitatively (Baker 2018).

We used *Sketch Engine* to run the keyness analysis, comparing the target corpus (our open question sub-corpus) against a reference corpus, in this case the English Web 2021 (enTenTen21) corpus, which comprises 52 billion words of English-language internet texts gathered between October 2021 and January 2022.[3] We chose enTenTen21 as our reference corpus because it is a very large general corpus, comprising samples of language about a broad range of topics, thus allowing us to identify the most distinctive words in our data. Sketch Engine uses the simple maths (Kilgarriff 2009) measure of effect size, which is used to rank each word in the target corpus according to the ratio of its relative frequency as compared to the relative frequency of the same word in the reference corpus.

We then examined the top 100 positive keywords in the target corpus, that is, those words with the biggest difference in relative frequency in favour of the target corpus, and therefore the words which are most distinctive in their rate of usage in our data. These keywords were then grouped according to thematic categories; this approach is a 'good starting point' for examination of discourses, as accessed through the analysis of collocations and concordance lines (Gillings et al. 2023, p. 36), which was the final step in our procedure as applied to keywords relevant to the emergent theme of participants' reported purposes of reading, including the use of reading as a coping strategy.

4   Analysis

4.1   Key Themes

The top 100 keywords in the open question sub-corpus are shown in Table 4.1, as grouped thematically (detailed frequency and keyness data is presented in Appendix 2).

Our analysis of the top 100 keywords reveals the salient topics that emerged in our participants' free-text responses to the open questions. This chapter focuses on some of the keywords in the PURPOSE group, as these point towards the reasons participants cited for reading during the first lockdown.

---

[3] See https://www.sketchengine.eu/ententen-english-corpus/.

4 READING AS A COPING STRATEGY   69

Table 4.1 Top 100 keywords thematically grouped

Thematic Group	Keyword (keyword rank)
Genre	post-apocalyptic (9), novels (11), genres (15), fiction (18), classics (19), non-fiction (20), thrillers (21), dystopian (25), romance (42), romances (43), apocalyptic (45), fanfiction (47), realist (55), poetry (62), detective (64), autobiographies (66), sff (68), depressing (71), nonfiction (74), fan-fiction (76), fantasy (90), biographies (93), scifi (95), graphic (97), blm (98)
Purpose	escapism (4), favourites (12), escapist (17), comforting (23), familiarity (24), concentrate (36), comfort (53), enjoyment (56), distractions (61), distracted (67), immerse (72), nostalgia (78), avoided (83), avoiding (86), distraction (91), concentrating (92), favourite (96)
Social	bookshops (65), whatsapp (10), commuting (22), bookclub (26), commute (30), dreamwidth (31), tumblr (32), instagram (41), fb (49), twitter (50), facebook (63), popsugar (79), discord (84), messenger (87), socialising (94)
Author	austen (13), pratchett (14), wodehouse (27), agatha (33), heyer (35), georgette (38), sayers (40), dickens (51), trollope (59), mantel (70), hobb (81), christie (82), atwood (85)
Mode	audiobooks (8), e-reader (16), kindle (28), ebooks (44), books (46), audiobook (52), ereader (75), hardbacks (77), e-books (80)
Practice	re-read (2), reread (3), re-reading (5), rereading (6), revisit (34), revisiting (48), reading (60)
Title	eyre (39), wuthering (57), middlemarch (58), gatsby (69), potter (73), omens (89), noughts (99)
Review site	goodreads (1), netgalley (37), librarything (100)
COVID-19	lockdown (7), furloughed (29), pre-lockdown (54)
Misc	eg (88)

4.2 A Sense of Security in a Time of Crisis

In this section, we examine how participants reported their use of reading as a positive coping strategy, analysing the reasons they provided for turning to reading, and drawing attention to the ways in which they framed their experiences, as accessed through the keywords.

A clear theme emerges when we focus on the keywords *comforting* (frequency = 60; 6.9 per 10,000 tokens) and *comfort* (frequency = 239; 27.6 per 10,000 tokens), which account for most instances of the headword COMFORT in the sub-corpus (299 out of 313). Most instances of *comforting* and *comfort* occur in responses to Questions 24e, 24d, and 17:

- Question 24e: *Since the start of the lockdown, why have you been re-reading books?* (96 hits; 164 per 10,000 tokens)
- Question 24d: *Before the lockdown, why did you re-read books?* (103 hits; 147 per 10,000 tokens)
- Question 17: *If you have been drawn to particular genres during the lockdown period, why do you think this is the case? Please give details.* (32 hits; 34 per 10,000 tokens)

These results highlight that 'reading as comfort' is a salient concept among participants when responding about why they read (or re-read) both in general but especially since the beginning of the lockdown. We explore how this concept is used by participants by examining their collocates. As in Chap. 3, these are measured using LogDice (Rychlý 2008), an association measure that favours 'collocates which occur exclusively in each other's company but do not have to be rare' (Brezina, 2018, p. 70). The top collocates of *comfort* and *comforting* are presented in Tables 4.2 and 4.3.[4]

The collocates *reading* and *read* refer predominantly to the practice of *comfort reading* and specific texts selected as *comfort reads*, respectively. Other collocates reveal a strong association between *comfort* and other nouns denoting mental/sensory experiences, predominantly *familiarity*, but also collocates like *enjoyment, relaxation, distraction,* and *nostalgia* (all of which but *relaxation* are also among the top 100 keywords). As demonstrated by the following examples, *comfort* is coordinated with *familiarity* in responses providing reasons for re-reading:

"Comfort books" so reread *The Hobbit* and *The Ring* as they're both favourite books and seeked some familiarity and comfort during uncertain time. (Participant 236)

Stick with the same routine for comfort and familiarity while not being able to control a lot of other issues. By reading what I want/like, I feel like I have control. (Participant 358)

Comfort and familiarity and wanting to get lost in familiar worlds and stories. (Participant 326)

---

[4] By default, Sketch Engine measures collocation irrespective of structural boundaries in the corpus (cf. Love et al. 2023). Therefore, several words that were identified as 'collocates', but actually occur in responses to adjacent survey questions, are omitted from this Table.

4 READING AS A COPING STRATEGY 71

Table 4.2 Top 20 collocates of *comfort* in the open question sub-corpus

Rank	Collocate	Co-occurrences	LogDice
1	familiarity	29	11.61
2	for	53	10.86
3	enjoyment	15	10.7
4	familiar	13	10.46
5	reading	46	10.42
6	reads	11	10.23
7	and	74	10.03
8	also	14	9.89
9	of	41	9.76
10	a	44	9.62
11	reread	9	9.62
12	in	28	9.6
13	distraction	6	9.55
14	old	7	9.49
15	re-reading	7	9.43
16	they	9	9.41
17	blanket	5	9.39
18	relaxation	5	9.36
19	's	9	9.2
20	classics	7	9.23

Table 4.3 Top 10 collocates of *comforting* in the open question sub-corpus

Rank	Collocate	Co-occurrences	LogDice
1	find	11	10.88
2	familiar	6	10.63
3	familiarity	5	10.34
4	nostalgia	3	10.19
5	is	11	9.76
6	there	3	9.36
7	something	4	9.35
8	's	6	9.31
9	very	3	9.21
10	it	12	8.99

Another collocate, *blanket*, draws us to the metaphorical *comfort blanket*, which is used by five participants to frame the role of reading as a form of security.

> Re-reading has been like a comfort blanket. Stories when you know what's coming are safe. (Participant 364)

Furthermore, the noun *nostalgia* is a top collocate of *comforting* and is a keyword in the open questions sub-corpus, occurring 24 times. Participants use *nostalgia* in the context of the comfort that is brought by returning to re-read texts, especially those from childhood.

> I've been particularly drawn into rereading my childhood favourites such as Pullman's *The Northern Lights* trilogy. Perhaps the nostalgia is comforting. (Participant 261)

> Children's books usually for the nostalgia or I'll re-read my favourites to cheer me up if I'm feeling low. (Participant 784)

> From a sense of nostalgia (for childhood favourites) and also so I could review them for my blog. (Participant 376)

> Nostalgia! I have been rereading a lot of historical fiction books that I loved during teen years. (Participant 74)

Participants' use of *nostalgia* is clearly associated with comfort and pleasure—therapeutic benefits of (re)reading. This contrasts with the use of *nostalgia* in public discourse; for example, in a corpus of UK press reporting, Marchi and Taylor (2023) found that *nostalgia* is increasingly evaluated negatively, as an intellectually feeble indulgence. However, it may be that the exceptional circumstances of the pandemic crisis gave rise to a sense of justification for taking part in activities that may otherwise have been considered indulgent. This is supported by evidence that re-reading a favourite familiar book induces higher feelings of nostalgia and narrative transportation, associated with social connectedness, relative to unfamiliar texts (Kneuer et al. 2022).

Grammatical collocates provide further insight; the prepositions *of* and *in* are used to ascribe *comfort* as an attribute of other noun phrases, which reinforces the framing of *comfort* as a form of security.

> The comfort and predictabilty of the familiar. (Participant 290)

Children's fiction for the comfort of the familiar. (Participant 808)

For a sense of comfort in the familiar and also as a means of escapism. (Participant 794)

Because I found comfort in the familiarity and knowing what would happen at the end. (Participant 57)

Comfort reading again. But maybe for a slightly different reason—there's been comfort in the certainty of certain books. In knowing there will be a resolution and a 'happy' ending. (Participant 582)

Similarly, forms of the copula verb BE (*is*, *'s*) allow us to access what is described by the adjective *comforting*, and in this context, *comforting* mostly refers to the *familiarity* of re-reading and related concepts, for example, *meeting again known characters* (Participant 215), *the promise of a happy ending* (Participant 285), and *to read something you know and enjoy* (Participant 145). Occasionally, *comforting* is used with BE in contexts unrelated to re-reading, suggesting that some participants associate comfort with the broader practice of reading:

Reading is comforting and I need all the comfort I can get at the moment. (Participant 771)

In one case, the comfort of reading extends to taking the opportunity to be reminded that the current situation could be worse, in comparison to negative historical events:

Historical—maybe puts the sweep of history into context. Also, it's strangely comforting to read about the grim past during a pandemic. (Participant 480)

In summary, the keywords *comfort*, *comforting*, *familiarity*, and *nostalgia* allow participants to talk about something they seek during the pandemic, namely security. The appeal of re-reading familiar texts, for instance, appears to be that it guarantees to provide readers with what they seek, which is a comforting and relaxing experience that provides distraction from the negative emotions associated with the COVID-19 pandemic, as summarised here:

For above reasons and also because it's very comforting to have a familiar read which you know is guaranteed to give you pleasure and take you to another place. (Participant 125)

Reading a new, unfamiliar text can, in contrast, be inferred to resemble something of a risk, as there is a chance that the text may not provide the experience readers are hoping for as a coping strategy in a time of crisis; indeed, wordforms of RISK appear five times in the free-text responses and are used to reinforce the notion of reading as a source of security, for example:

> Not a good time to risk not liking something new. Would rather go with what I know I will enjoy. (Participant 358)

For many, the pandemic created an unprecedented and long period of instability and uncertainty. The desire for a sense of security, something that the public sought during this period, meant that what is in 'normal times' an appealing attribute of reading for pleasure—'the novelty of a new book' (Kneuer et al. 2022, p. 2)—was less desirable, overridden by readers opting to return to texts they know, seeking comfort in nostalgia.

4.3 Distraction from Reality

In the previous section, we demonstrated that the concept of *familiarity* of reading material (a keyword in its own right) is strongly associated with *comfort*. However, the familiarity that participants value is conditional; it is nostalgic familiarity with childhood memories or otherwise 'happier times'. As we explore in this section, keywords relating to escapism and distraction reveal that the desire for familiarity does not extend to texts that are too familiar to the present; texts that remind readers too much of the pandemic context are strongly dispreferred. We have discussed this in terms of genre avoidance in Chap. 2, but here we turn to broader themes relating to the more general practice of reading as a coping strategy.

The concept of escapism is indexed by keywords *escapism* and *escapist*. As discussed in Chap. 2, escapism is a salient concept in responses to questions about genre, and the same is true of responses to all open questions more broadly, as it also appears in responses to questions about other topics including re-reading and reading quantity. In total, wordforms of ESCAPE occur 191 times in the open question sub-corpus (22 times per 10,000 tokens). In addition to *escapism* and *escapist*, the sub-corpus contains the wordforms *escape* and *escaping*, with frequencies as detailed in Table 4.4.

ESCAPE is a material process (Halliday and Matthiessen 2014) involving the movement of an agent from a source and/or towards a goal. In the open question sub-corpus, we identified the sources and goals of ESCAPE, as used metaphorically, to explore how the role of reading as a coping strategy is framed.

4 READING AS A COPING STRATEGY   75

Table 4.4 Wordforms of ESCAPE in the open question sub-corpus

Wordform	Frequency
escapism (noun)	85
escape (verb)	43
escape (noun)	36
escapist (adjective)	22
escaping (verb)	5
Total	*191*

The source of ESCAPE is identified in the direct object of the transitive verb or in a prepositional phrase, headed by *from*, which modifies intransitive verbs and nouns. Using Sketch Engine's *Word Sketch* feature, across all forms of ESCAPE, we found 15 sources encoded in direct objects and 15 sources encoded in *from*-phrases. The most commonly cited source (n = 11) is *reality*, followed by other sources indicating the current situation (*situation, today, events, news, current affairs, real life, world*) and terms relating to poor mental health (*misery, anxiety, stress, thought*). Only one source refers explicitly to the pandemic (*lockdown*).

> More non-fiction including biographies, as a means of escaping my own reality and living vicariously through other's' (Participant 162)

> Those fantasy storylines are bittersweet and allow me to escape our current situation even for a brief moment. (Participant 284)

> Detective novels—familiarity and mental stimulation Medieval poetry—a chance to escape from current stresses and situations [...] (Participant 459)

> Escapism from depressing news on tv and on social media. (Participant 651)

The goal of ESCAPE is identified in prepositional phrases, headed by *into, to,* or *in*, which modify intransitive verbs and nouns. These provide an insight into the metaphorical 'destination' of participants' escapism as facilitated by reading. We found nine instances of explicitly stated goals of ESCAPE, four of which are *world*, followed by *safe place, setting, experiences, earlier period in history,* and *book*.

> I like to have a story to immerse myself in, now is a particularly good time to escape to another world! (Participant 637)

> I've read a lot of Stephen King's short stories. The genre previously held no appeal for me and I've not read King before. I can only think it's a form of escapism into fictional worlds. (Participant 449)

> To escape to a safe place with characters I know and problems with solutions. (Participant 451)

The adjective *escapist* is interesting because it provides an insight into how the concept of escapism is used evaluatively. Some participants imply that their interest in reading for escapism is exceptional to the circumstances of the pandemic and not representative of their usual reading habits. The adjective *escapist* is quantified by *more* (n = 5), suggesting by way of a relative scale of escapism, that they have turned to escapist literature during the pandemic.

> I have sought out slightly more escapist narratives. (Participant 666)

Furthermore, adverbials (*while, at the moment, though, instead*) are used to qualify that exceptional, contextually motivated nature of participants' interest in escapism.

> While what I've been reading feels escapist, it still feels proximate to our lived experience. (Participant 120)

> I like anything that's escapist at the moment—nothing that reminds me of normal life. (Participant 43)

> Fantasy and other escapist genres are appealing at the moment, it makes a nice change from the real world drama. (Participant 674)

> I've found myself more drawn to fantasy which was a genre I generally avoided before. I really like the escapist quality to it though during lockdown. (Participant 212)

> Instead, I've been drawn to escapist novels that immerse me in another world that isn't ending. (Participant 485)

While the majority of participants who mention escapism discuss how this is something they have sought through their reading practice, some participants reject or contest escapism, using negation of *escapist* to explain that using reading to escape from reality is not something they feel helps them to cope.

Table 4.5 Wordforms of DISTRACT in the open question sub-corpus

Wordform	Frequency
distraction (noun)	46
distracted (verb, adjective)	33
distract (verb)	6
distractable (adjective)	1
distracting (adjective)	1
Total	87

I've been struggling to concentrate and seeking more escapist entertainment. For me reading is too close to reality and not escapist. (Participant 722)

Fairy tales should be, in a proportion, a replica or a mirroring of reality and shouldn't be necessarily escapist literature, but at the same time, they give you a morale which is not applicable for the current situation. I cannot identify with it because the outside world is making me feel anxious and afraid for the future. (Participant 219)

Another relevant set of keywords are wordforms of DISTRACT: *distractions*, *distracted*, and *distraction*. Wordforms of DISTRACT occur 87 times (10 per 10,000 tokens) in the open question sub-corpus (Table 4.5), most frequently in response to Questions 6a (31) and 5a (24), which ask participants to elaborate on their responses to closed questions about reading speed and time spent reading.

In the sub-corpus, plural noun *distractions* is often (n = 20) quantified, mostly by minimisers *less* (10) and *fewer* (8). In these cases, participants attribute having *less/fewer distractions* as a reason for reading more during the pandemic.

More time, and less distractions—without live sport or events to go to, books are being read in a much quicker time. (Participant 396)

However, participants who reported reading less/slower than usual during the lockdown cited having more distractions as the reason for this, highlighting the heterogeneity of lockdown experiences. Using Sketch Engine's *Word Sketch* feature, we identified 11 instances of DISTRACT with explicitly stated causes, expressed as the unwanted agent of distraction (subject of the verb or prepositional *by*-phrase). The unwanted agents of distraction are social media (*Twitter, my phone/laptop*), children (*my kids*), and the broader current situation (*news, things, activities, and events*).

I'm more prone to being distracted by my phone/laptop, specifically social media. I haven't maintained dedicated reading time during each day. (Participant 224)

In other cases, reading (e.g. *book, novel*) is framed as the (welcome) agent of distraction from the sources that would otherwise cause a (unwelcome) distraction, as indicated by the prepositional *from*-phrase. The sources from which reading is a welcome agent of distraction are the *the pandemic, the drudgery of life in lockdown, horrible reality, bad news,* and *work*.

I have found books a welcome distraction from bad news and the worrying news about Covid-19. Reading has always been my primary form of entertainment, and as I can't do some of the other things I normally enjoy, I have more time to read. (Participant 306)

This shows that, for some, the pandemic is framed as having removed distractions, thus creating more time for recreational reading. For others, reading itself is a distraction, but one that is evaluated positively, as it is framed as a useful coping strategy that functions to distract readers from the negative feelings brought upon by the pandemic.

Overall, keywords associated with ESCAPE and DISTRACT are useful access points for participants' reflections on the role that reading plays in helping them to cope in this time of crisis. The specific sources of escape and causes of distraction are not often stated explicitly; of the 191 instances of ESCAPE in the sub-corpus, only a minority have an explicitly stated source, and even fewer a goal. Most uses of ESCAPE do not specify a source or a goal, but rather convey the broader notion of using reading to escape an unspecified but possibly implied situation (for instance, using the intransitive verb with no modifying prepositional phrase, e.g. *Prefer to read alternative world fiction to escape*, Participant 505). Similarly, most instances of DISTRACT are not explicitly specified; rather, they more generally refer to the effect that reading has on readers' mental state (e.g. *I like the distraction of a novel*, Participant 408). This suggests that the salient conceptions of escapism and distraction in our data are motivated by a desire for any type of transportation (Gerrig 1993) from what is mentally preoccupying readers. While, in many instances, this is not explicitly stated, the examples that do provide elaboration offer a clear indication of the therapeutic role of reading in the lockdown. Reading is used as an 'escape' and a 'distraction' to transport readers from the reality of the lockdown situation, be it from negative thoughts, worrying current events, or the monotony of the lockdown experience.

5 Conclusion

In this chapter, we have explored how salient terms in the free-text responses to the survey's open questions reflect participants' use of reading as a coping strategy during the first lockdown. We have necessarily taken an inductive approach to the topic of reading to cope, as participants' reflections on this topic were not directly elicited, nor were they often explicitly framed in terms of how reading helps one to 'cope'. Instead, we have identified potential signposts towards relevant themes within responses to questions that are not ostensibly 'about' coping strategies, but nonetheless revealing of the therapeutic motivations for reading during the lockdown. We have explored two emergent themes: the use of reading as a source of comfort and security and the use of reading as a distraction from reality. Reading can provide comfort through revisiting and re-reading stories that are familiar, nostalgic, and, crucially, situationally disconnected to the current crisis. Reading can provide security through the choice to re-read known texts, thereby guaranteeing that that text provides the emotional experience that the reader seeks. Reading can provide escapism by distracting the mind from the present situation.

Clearly, our participants reported a therapeutic benefit in returning to familiar favourites, especially texts enjoyed during childhood, as a coping strategy during a time of crisis. On the basis of Zajonc's familiarity principle (1968), whereby there is a positive correlation between repeated exposure to an item and enhanced for that item, Kneuer et al. (2022) found that re-reading a favourite book elicits greater 'social connectedness', an index of wellbeing that involves 'perceptions of social bonds, attachment security, interpersonal competence, and social support' (Hepper et al. 2012, p. 104). Furthermore, re-reading childhood novels and poetry can be used as a means of guaranteeing that the content aligns with the needs of the reader, needs that are motivated by the nature of the crisis.

In this chapter, our use of keyness analysis as an inductive approach to the exploration of our data has both reinforced the salience of the themes already discussed in previous chapters, as well as revealing framings that help us to better interpret of the experiences of our participants. The specific importance and value placed on the practice of re-reading, and especially its role in helping readers to 'escape' reality, is explored in further depth in Chap. 5.

References

Altmann, U., I.C. Bohrn, O. Lubrich, W. Menninghaus, and A.M. Jacobs. 2012. The power of emotional valence-from cognitive to affective processes in reading. *Frontiers in Human Neuroscience* 6: 6. https://doi.org/10.3389/fnhum.2012.00192.

Baker, Paul. 2018. Keywords: Signposts to objectivity? The corpus linguistics discourse: In honour of Wolfgang Teubert. In *Studies in corpus linguistics*, ed. Anna Čermáková and Michaela Mahlberg, vol. 87, 77–94. Amsterdam: John Benjamins Publishing Company. https://doi.org/10.1075/scl.87.04bak.

Bate, Jonathan, and Andrew Schuman. 2016. Books do furnish a mind: The art and science of bibliotherapy. *Lancet* 387: 742–743.

Brewster, Liz. 2016. More benefit from a well-stocked library than a well-stocked pharmacy: How do readers use books as therapy? In *Plotting the Reading experience: Theory/practice/politics*, ed. Paulette M. Rothbauer, Kjell Ivar Skjerdingstad, Lynne E.F. McKechnie, and Knut Oterholm, 167–182. Waterloo, Ontario: Wilfred Laurier University Press.

Brezina, Vaclav. 2018. *Statistics in corpus linguistics: A practical guide*. Cambridge: Cambridge University Press.

Dewan, Pauline. 2022. Leisure Reading as a mindfulness activity: The implications for academic reference librarians. *The Reference Librarian* 64 (1): 1–16. https://doi.org/10.1080/02763877.2022.2156968.

Gabrielatos, Costas. 2018. Keyness analysis: Nature, metrics and techniques. In *Corpus approaches to discourse: A critical review*, ed. Charlotte Taylor and Anna Marchi, 252–258. London: Routledge.

Gellatly, Judith, Peter Bower, Sue Hennessy, David Richards, Simon Gilbody, and Karina Lovell. 2007. What makes self help interventions effective in the management of depressive symptoms? Meta-analysis and meta-regression. *Psychological Medicine* 37: 1217–1228.

Gerrig, Richard. 1993. *Experiencing narrative worlds: On the psychological activities of reading*. New Haven: Yale University Press.

Gillings, Mathew, Gerlinde Mautner, and Paul Baker. 2023. *Corpus-assisted discourse studies*. Cambridge: Cambridge University Press.

Gray, Ellie, Gundi Kiemle, Philip Davis, and Josei Billington. 2015. Making sense of mental health difficulties through live reading: An interpretative phenomenological analysis of the experience of being in a reader group. *Arts Health* 3015: 1–14.

Green, Kelda. 2020. *Rethinking therapeutic reading: Lessons from Seneca, Montaigne, Wordsworth and George Eliot*. London: Anthem Press.

Green, Melanie C., and Timothy C. Brock. 2000. The role of transportation in the persuasiveness of public narratives. *Journal of Personality and Social Psychology* 79 (5): 701–721. https://doi.org/10.1037/0022-3514.79.5.701.

Halliday, Michael A.K., and Christian M.I.M. Matthiessen. 2014. *Halliday's introduction to functional grammar*. 4th ed. London: Routledge.

Hepper, Erica G., Timothy D. Ritchie, Constantine Sedikides, and Tim Wildschut. 2012. Odyssey's end: Lay conceptions of nostalgia reflect its original homeric meaning. *Emotion* 12 (1): 102–119. https://doi.org/10.1037/a0025167.

Johnson, Dan R. 2012. Transportation into a story increases empathy, prosocial behavior, and perceptual bias toward fearful expressions. *Personality and Individual Differences* 52 (2): 150–155.

Kate Nash Literary Agency. 2020. The three key trends to emerge in reading during lockdown. https://katenashlit.co.uk/2020/05/15/the-three-key-trends-to-emerge-in-reading-during-lockdown/. Accessed 27 August 2023.

Kidd, David Comer, and Emanuele Castano. 2013. Reading literary fiction improves theory of mind. *Science* 342: 377–380. https://doi.org/10.1126/science.1239918.

———. 2017. Different stories: How levels of familiarity with literary and genre fiction relate to mentalizing. *Psychology of Aesthetics, Creativity, and the Arts* 11: 474–486.

Kilgarriff, Adam. 2009. Simple maths for keywords. In *Proceedings of corpus linguistics conference CL2009*, ed. Michaela Mahlberg, Victorina González-Díaz, and Catherine Smith. Liverpool: University of Liverpool. https://www.sketchengine.eu/wp-content/uploads/2015/04/2009-Simple-maths-for-keywords.pdf.

Kneuer, Margaret A., Jeffrey D. Green, and Athena H. Cairo. 2022. Psychological effects of reading: The role of nostalgia in re-reading favorite books. *The Journal of Social Psychology*. https://doi.org/10.1080/00224545.2022.2151403.

Lee, Kang, Victoria Talwar, Anjanie McCarthy, Ilana Ross, Angela Evans, and Cindy Arruda. 2014. Can classic moral stories promote honesty in children? *Psychological Science* 25 (8): 1630–1636.

Levine, Shelby L., Sarah Cherrier, Anne C. Holding, and Richard Koestner. 2020. For the love of reading: Recreational reading reduces psychological distress in college students and autonomous motivation is the key. *Journal of American College Health, Advance Online Publication* 70 (1): 158–164. https://doi.org/10.1080/07448481.2020.1728280.

Love, Robbie, Isobelle Clarke, and Mark McGlashan. 2023. Evaluating collocation in spoken dialogic corpora. In *Corpus linguistics international conference 2023*. Lancaster: Lancaster University. https://research.aston.ac.uk/en/activities/evaluating-collocation-in-spoken-dialogic-corpora.

Mackiewicz, Jo, and Isabelle Thompson. 2016. Adding quantitative corpus-driven analysis to qualitative discourse analysis: Determining the aboutness of writing Center talk. *The Writing Center Journal* 35 (3): 187–225.

Mar, Raymond, K. Keith Oatley, Jacob Hirsh, Jennifer dela Paz, and Jordan B. Peterson. 2006. Bookworms versus nerds: Exposure to fiction versus non-fiction, divergent associations with social ability, and the simulation of fictional social worlds. *Journal of Research in Personality* 40: 694–712. https://doi.org/10.1016/j.jrp.2005.08.002.

Marchi, Anna, and Charlotte Taylor. 2023. Is nostalgia what it used to be? The rhetorical functions of 'nostalgia' and 'nostalgic' over time. In *Corpus linguistics international conference 2023*. Lancaster: Lancaster University.

McEnery, Tony, and Vaclav Brezina. 2022. *Fundamental principles of corpus linguistics*. Cambridge: Cambridge University Press.

McNichol, Sarah, and Liz Brewster, eds. 2018. *Bibliotherapy*. London: Facet Publishing.

Oatley, Keith. 1994. A taxonomy of the emotions of literary response and a theory of identification in fictional narrative. *Poetics* 23 (1–2): 53–74.

———. 2016. Fiction: Simulation of social worlds. *Trends in Cognitive Sciences* 20 (8): 618–662.

Orr, Gregory. 2002. *Poetry as survival*. Athens, GA: University of Georgia Press.

Partington, Alan, Alison Duguid, and Charlotte Taylor. 2013. *Patterns and meanings in discourse: Theory and practice in corpus-assisted discourse studies (CADS)*. Amsterdam: John Benjamins.

Rychlý, Pavel. 2008. A lexicographer-friendly association score. Proc. 2nd workshop on recent advances in Slavonic natural languages processing. *RASLAN* 2: 6–9. https://www.sketchengine.eu/wp-content/uploads/2015/03/Lexicographer-Friendly_2008.pdf.

Tognini-Bonelli, Elena. 2001. *Corpus linguistics at work*. Amsterdam: John Benjamins.

Topping, Keith, and Christina Clark. 2021. *What and how kids are reading: The book-reading behaviours of pupils in pandemic times: Pandemic edition*. London: Renaissance Learning.

Waller, Alison, and Rita J. Dashwood. 2022. Reading for normal: Young people and YA fiction in the time of Covid-19. *Mémoires du livre/Studies in Book Culture* 13 (2): 1–36.

Wilkinson, Katherine. 2020. Reading in lockdown: mental wellbeing. https://www.scottishbooktrust.com/articles/reading-in-lockdown-mental-wellbeing. Accessed 27 August 2023.

Zajonc, Robert B. 1968. Attitudinal effects of mere exposure. *Journal of Personality and Social Psychology* 9 (2, Pt.2): 1–27. https://doi.org/10.1037/h002.

CHAPTER 5

Re-reading in the Pandemic

Abstract This chapter examines how participants in our data reported returning to books that they had previously read which offered familiarity, reliability, and nostalgia and thus provided a coping mechanism. The chapter begins with a survey of the latest research in re-reading as a phenomenon, drawing on theoretical and empirical studies that have sought to explore why people re-read and the personal benefits of re-reading fiction. We then turn to our data to explore the reasons participants gave us for returning to particular books or reading habits from before the pandemic, and we examine the ways in which they talked about the emotional, immersive, and parasocial aspects of re-reading. We then look at the specific ways that they explain their reasons for re-reading books. In this latter respect, we examine the metaphors, generally concerned with reassurance and the emotional support brought about by returning to familiar storylines, that readers draw on to frame their re-reading choices and to reveal their motivations for re-reading.

Keywords Re-reading • Readers • Emotions • Immersion • Metaphor

© The Author(s), under exclusive license to Springer Nature Switzerland AG 2024
A. Boucher et al., *Reading Habits in the COVID-19 Pandemic*, https://doi.org/10.1007/978-3-031-52753-1_5

1 Introduction

This chapter extends the discussion in Chap. 4 by examining how participants in our data reported returning to books that they had previously read which offer familiarity, predictability, nostalgia, and escape. For many, early lockdown life in the UK was filled with social and physical restrictions which engendered a pervasive feeling of monotony and repetition in everyday life. The closure of libraries and book shops removed the option to physically browse for books which restricted access to new reading materials. At the same time, many wished to save money. These latter factors meant that, for some, returning to the bookshelf at home to re-read an old book was an inviting option. Reports during this time suggested that people were revisiting familiar stories in other ways. For example, an increase in traffic to fanfiction sites, which offer readers 'the soothing experience of new stories set in recognizable places with characters we already know' (Wendell 2020), was identified, while others spoke of revisiting narratives across other media such as TV (Sillett 2020; Andrews 2021).

In this chapter, we explore how our participants framed their motivations for and experiences of re-reading during the early lockdown. We begin with a survey of the latest research in re-reading as a phenomenon, drawing on theoretical and empirical studies that have sought to explore why people re-read and the personal benefits of re-reading fiction. The chapter then turns to the dataset to explore the reasons participants identified for returning to particular books, from before the pandemic and since the start of the lockdown, and the participants' reflections on changes to re-reading habits are also considered. Through a stylistic application of Conceptual Metaphor Theory (Lakoff and Johnson 1980), the analysis examines how the re-readers 'frame' (Semino et al. 2016, p. 18) their reported experiences. In particular, it considers the ways in which they talk about the emotional, immersive, and parasocial aspects of re-reading at the start of the pandemic.

2 Context

2.1 Re-reading

Re-reading a text, albeit through second, third, or multiple readings, invites varied experiences. The text remains the same, while the attitudinal, social, or contextual stance of the reader will have altered. Significantly, readers' knowledge of the text or story will uncover or modify perceptions and interpretations. As Iser (1989, p. 10) notes,

> The increased information that now overshadows the text provides possibilities of combination that were obscured in the first reading. Familiar occurrences now tend to appear in a new light and seem to be at times corrected, at times enriched. But for all that, nothing is formulated in the text itself; rather, the reader himself produces these innovative readings.

Re-reading is a process that therefore places primary focus on individualised reader inference and experience. Though retaining this focus on reader experience, in empirical studies of literature, re-reading is defined and applied in different ways. Harrison and Nuttall (2018) overview of the term (and cognate labels *re-read(s), reread(s), second reading(s)*) and its treatment in stylistics, in particular, found varied uses that captured, among others, its appearance in a literary or theoretical context where people talk of *re-reading the work of a particular scholar* and where it is often used to suggest the production of an alternative interpretation (which Nuttall and Harrison differentiate as 're-interpretation', 178). Re-reading can also be used to describe an *experimental reader protocol*: researchers may ask participants to read and then re-read a text to capture differences in first and second readings (Harrison and Nuttall 2019, 2021; Xue et al. 2020) or to explore how re-reading might influence experiences of literariness where linguistic choices or patterns are foregrounded (Dixon et al. 1993; Sanford and Sturt 2002; Bray 2007; Hakemulder 2007). Following the work of Harrison and Nuttall (2018), in this chapter, we examine re-reading in the pandemic as a *reading habit*: those occasions where readers choose to return to a book previously read as part of their everyday engagement with texts. With notable exceptions such as Waller's (2020) study of re-reading childhood books and Spacks' (2011) autobiographical reflection on re-reading for pleasure, re-reading as a habit has hitherto not been extensively explored.

In a contemporary psychology study that was curtailed by the start of the pandemic, Ministero et al. (2021) explore re-reading as a means for people to fulfil unmet social needs. They identify it as a habit 'especially common among those who desire social connection but feel like their social needs are not met in their daily lives' (1). They argue that re-readers are not those that necessarily seek predictability in all aspects of life, but rather that the act fulfils a psychological function that offers 'an emotionally safe way to feel socially connected' (1). Re-readers are able to enact relationships with characters and practice 'mind-modelling' (Stockwell 2009) the characters' thoughts and actions, in an environment where there are no negative repercussions, or unknown or unwelcome surprises awaiting their friends. This idea of safe or risk-free social connection aligns with other views of reading as a 'playground' in which readers can vicariously road test and refine their socio-cognitive skills (Boyd 2009). In their study of 671 participants, Ministero et al. found that re-reading is connected with particular personality traits: for example, it predicted higher levels of personal distress and negative emotionality. Their findings suggested that re-reading is 'associated with anxious-preoccupied and fearful-avoidant attachment styles' (9), and, further, 'that the tendency to reread is associated with a curious and creative but perhaps more solitary personality' (9).

The data collection for Ministero et al's project was disrupted by the start of the COVID-19 pandemic, and the team identified that the impact of this on re-reading motivations and experiences would make for an interesting and topical further study. The results of their study certainly raise questions about the significance of contextual factors on readers' habits and preferences; in particular, the extent to which the forced isolation and higher anxiety state induced by the pandemic simulates or exacerbates those psychological factors in a way that is external to a person's natural personality traits.

2.2 Metaphors for (Re-)Reading

As we highlight in Chaps. 3 and 4, readers often draw on different conceptual metaphors (Lakoff and Johnson 1980) to frame their reading experiences. Stockwell (2009) summarises these metaphors as follows:

- READING IS TRANSPORT (Gerrig 1993; e.g. *This book transports us to another time and place*);
- READING IS CONTROL (e.g. *I could not stop reading this book!*);
- READING IS INVESTMENT (e.g. *This book was so rewarding*).

In a study of reader reviews of the contemporary Young Adult novel *Twilight*, Nuttall and Harrison (2020) find that previous claims about the high frequencies of these types of metaphors used by readers are supported in reader review data, but they also note that other novel metaphors, which include those relating to EATING and ADDICTION, are apparent in reader discourse. In fact, their study of 200 reviews of the 1-star and 5-star conditions identifies that READING IS TRANSPORT, READING IS CONTROL, AND READING IS EATING are the most frequent reading metaphors among both positive and negative ratings. Drawing on concepts from Cognitive Grammar (Langacker 2008), Nuttall and Harrison find that readers reveal their construal of reader agency and (dis)empowerment through their linguistic choices and localised framings.

As we also highlighted in Chap. 3, many readers experienced reading in the pandemic as a process that was volitionally activated, or as something that impacted on them with minimal effort on their part. We hypothesise that re-reading metaphors are likely to show the same embodied metaphors as the conceptualisations of reading listed above, but through different constructions and mappings.

3 Methodology

In this chapter, we examine data drawn from Question 24 in the *Aston Lockdown Reading Survey Corpus*. The first questions asked whether people re-read books generally (24) and then during the lockdown specifically (24a). For those who responded that they did re-read, a series of follow-up questions were presented, which included the following:

24b. Which books (e.g. specific titles) or types of books (e.g. genres) do you re-read normally?
24c. Which books (e.g. specific titles) or types of books (e.g. genres) have you been re-reading during the lockdown?
24d. Before the lockdown, why did you re-read books?
24e. Since the start of the lockdown, why have you been re-reading books?

These questions were designed to capture readers' reflections on their prior re-reading habits, and how these might have altered since the lockdown. A summary of the data (Tables 5.1 and 5.2) shows that most of the surveyed participants (just over 85%) are re-readers to some extent, with 20% categorising themselves as frequent re-readers, 37% as occasional re-readers, and 28% as re-reading rarely.

Participants were offered a free-text response for each question. One hundred and twenty-eight participants answered 'Never' and therefore did not contribute to the remaining questions. The free-text answers for the

Table 5.1 Summary of responses to Question 24

Option	Number and percentage of responses selecting option
Yes, frequently	174 (20.3%)
Yes, sometimes	318 (37.1%)
Yes, rarely	237 (27.7%)
Never	128 (14.9%)

Table 5.2 Summary of responses to Question 24a

Option	Number and percentage of responses selecting option
About the same as I normally would	381 (52.6%)
Less than I normally would	148 (20.4%)
More than I normally would	196 (27%)

responses to the follow-up questions on book and genre choices (24b–24c) answered by the other 732 participants were sorted in Sketch Engine and organised by the top ten recurring keywords for each question. To capture the more nuanced descriptions of motivations for and changes in re-reading practice in the responses to questions (24d–e), the remaining data forming a sub-corpus of 12,878 tokens were uploaded to NVivo, coded for recurring themes, and then further coded for recurring metaphors across the themes. These codes form the basis of the analysis in Sect. 4.

Unsurprisingly, the re-readers acknowledged that all motivations for re-reading are underpinned by pursuit of *enjoyment*. Re-readers report specifically looking to recapture the same sense of enjoyment a second time round, and this prioritisation of re-reading for pleasure supports observations made in other research on re-reading motivations (e.g. Jeffries 2001; Harrison and Nuttall 2018). Accounts of re-reading as an enjoyable experience crossed over with all other codes that appeared across the responses, which included (in descending order of frequency):

1. *Comfort and familiarity* (e.g. 'I take a lot of comfort in re-reading familiar stories', Participant 462).
2. *Comprehension*[1] (e.g. 'To clarify points which I had forgotten', Participant 446).

[1] Re-reading for comprehension is referred to as an 'epistemic rereading stance' by Doche and Ross (2023).

3. *Emotional resonance* (e.g. 'To relive the same emotions I gained from reading certain books', Participant 809).
4. *Transportation* (e.g. 'I re-read books because I love the story and they easily transport me to a different world', Participant 650).
5. *Aesthetic appreciation* (e.g. 'To remind myself of great writing', Participant 165).

The top three key drivers for changes in re-reading behaviour since the start of the pandemic relate to the same motivations as listed above, but emphasise different aspects of those motivations. For example, the participants described how they re-read during lockdown as part of their desire for familiarity, but more specifically out of a desire for comfort, for predictability, and for a story to have a known, and happy, resolution. Equally, the participants reflected on their desire for transportation as part of their wider re-reading practice, but that lockdown invited, more specifically, a desire to re-read for escape.

4 ANALYSIS

4.1 *Which Books and Genres Were Re-read?*

The re-readers were asked to identify which types of books (genres) and specific titles they re-read. Table 5.3 below shows the most frequent responses for before and since the start of the lockdown.

Table 5.3 Which books do you re-read? Summary of top participant responses for before and since lockdown

	Before lockdown	Since lockdown
Genres	1. Classics 2. Fantasy 3. Romance 4. Poetry 5. Crime	1. Romance 2. Poetry 3. Classics 4. Crime 5. Fantasy
Authors	1. Austen 2. Dickens 3. Pratchett	1. Austen 2. Christie 3. Pratchett
Books	1. *Harry Potter* 2. *Lord of the Rings* 3. *Pride and Prejudice*	1. *Harry Potter* 2. *Twilight* 3. *The Great Gatsby*

Before the lockdown, the participants reported classics as the most re-read genre, with genre fiction—and fantasy, romance, and crime, in particular—also popular genres for re-reading (see Chap. 2 for an extended discussion of sought and avoided genres). Since the start of the pandemic, the same genres are identified by the re-readers, but with a slightly different emphasis: romance and poetry more sought within this early lockdown period. This propensity towards classics is similarly observed in findings from a later lockdown, where Davies et al. (2022) found that readers discussed a preference for re-reading classics for a physical as much as an experiential reason; people are more likely to have copies of classic books on their bookshelves. Preferences for the other genres identified are likely to be connected with the motivations of re-readers to experience predictability and escapism, especially given the more formulaic scripts associated with these genres.

Accordingly, the authors and specific titles referenced by the re-readers are representative of their genre preferences. Austen and Dickens are canonical writers synonymous with classics, Pratchett with fantasy, and Christie with detective fiction. That Austen remains the most mentioned author aligns with previous research by White (2018) that observes how Austen was also a popular choice for reading during World War Two, and the general preference for readers to take refuge in 'Austenian idylls' during times of trauma. The specific titles identified by the re-readers similarly align, with some of these titles featuring elements across more than one of the preferred genres: *Twilight*, for example, blends both fantasy and romance; *Pride and Prejudice* is similarly a classic that is focused on the courtship of Elizabeth Bennett and Mr. Darcy, and so on. Like another contemporary study by Harrison and Nuttall (2018), *Harry Potter* (1997–2007) was identified as the most popular re-read title and forms an established, shared cultural reference point for contemporary readers. Again, this preference may relate to other re-reading motivations. Ministero et al. (2021, p. 3), for example, argue that reading this particular series offers parasocial benefits in that 'those who read Harry Potter may feel as if they are part of the wizard community', while its mainstream nature and its adaptation across modes and forms offer an accessible point of connection for those who experience higher parasocial relationships with the series' characters (Ingram and Luckett 2019).

4.2 Re-reading for Familiarity, Comfort, and Emotional Support

In this section, we explore the participants' 'framings' (Semino et al. 2016) and conceptual blends of the two most frequent metaphors that appeared across the data codes, RE-READING IS A RELATIONSHIP and RE-READING IS A JOURNEY,[2] through a cognitive stylistic perspective. Semino et al.'s (2016) exploration of metaphor framing examines the entities, roles, and relations that are focused in the source domain scenario (Musolff 2006), as well as the relative 'agency, (dis)empowerment, evaluations, and emotions' (2016, p. 18) arising from discussions of metaphors in context. Here our analysis explores the ways that the readers framed (2016) their experiences and what this suggests about conceptualisations of re-reading in the pandemic.

4.2.1 RE-READING IS A RELATIONSHIP

As part of their descriptions of re-reading for familiarity and comfort, the participants acknowledged the existing relationships and friendships they held with particular fictional characters, as in the following examples:

I enjoy revisiting characters and remembering scenes I love. (Participant 222)

Because i [sic] missed the characters and the plots, and how the books made me feel. (Participant 296)

There is a security in familiarity and good novels can provide that. I find it enjoyable to share a space with characters I've met before. (I am a rational person really!) (Participant 377)

Fondness for the characters. (Participant 509)

I re-read to re-enter a world I have enjoyed and to reconnect with those characters. (Participant 567)

---

[2] Other recurring metaphors in the coded data frame reading as a valuable resource. In the responses for *re-reading for aesthetic appreciation*, for example, writing and texts are framed as valuable items that yield richness or depth, or that are treated by readers as valuable aesthetic artefacts (Miall 2006; Miall and Kuiken 1994). The value metaphor for reading also appeared in re-reading for comprehension, where many re-readers acknowledged the need to 'get more out of a book', but at the same time frequently modalised their responses of this type of re-reading as a duty or obligation (e.g., I've *had to study* them for my work, see also Harrison and Nuttall 2018).

Re-readers acknowledged an emotional response to their friendship with fictional characters, who are perceived as familiar friends who are 'missed', who they wish to 'reconnect with' and for whom they feel 'fondness'. At the same time, re-readers also discussed these characters in terms of occupying a physical location that endures through time. They are people who we might 'revisit', and with whom we can physically 'share a space'. While the sense of 'revisiting' a fictional world evokes a transportation metaphor, these conceptualisations of *characters as friends* are not entirely metaphorical. Extensive critical literature on characterisation argues that readers use the same mental faculties for modelling characters as they do real people, though such relationships are more attenuated (Culpeper 2001; Palmer 2004; Zunshine 2006). Such descriptions demonstrate re-readers' experiences of 'narrative collective assimilation', which is a process that 'leads people to psychologically become part of a social group within a story, even temporarily adopting traits and signal belongingness within a fictional group. People may reread books in order to revisit these collectives that they have psychologically joined' (Ministero et al. 2021, p. 3). In revisiting these collectives, re-readers construe these fictional characters as part of their social network, albeit as friends who are more distanced in their axial relationship within it.

In contrast, other re-readers conceptualised the text or book itself as the target domain, and instead framed their response through a BOOKS ARE FRIENDS metaphor:

> For the pleasure of a familiar companion. (Participant 113)

> It's like meeting up with an old friend or lover. (Participant 139)

> To re-acquaint myself with them. (Participant 164)

> [C]omfort and the joy of visiting old friends. (Participant 183)

> When I run out of new books and am waiting for a delivery, I return to my old friends. (Participant 448)

> Re reading a good book can be like re connecting with an old friend. (Participant 644)

The framings of BOOKS ARE FRIENDS is an instantiation of the superordinate READING IS A RELATIONSHIP metaphor (Nuttall and Harrison 2020, p. 51), with the text conceptualised as a person (Booth 1980, p. 6; Holland 1988,

p. 159) who is 'a familiar companion' and an 'old friend'. Compared to the examples of characters are friends from the re-readers earlier, this framing increases in metaphoricity: the 'scope' (Langacker 2008) of the target domain is widened from a fictional character within the story to include the book or text more holistically with the text is attributed with human-like qualities. Some re-readers evoked this metaphor more schematically through their framing of verb processes (they describe, for example, acts of reacquainting, revisiting, reencountering, reconnecting), and through conceptualising themselves as the initiator, the 'agent' (Langacker 2008; see Chap. 3) of the action. Other re-readers framed this metaphor more explicitly through simile constructions (e.g. 'like meeting up with an old friend') and through the evocative identification of the 'old friend' status of the text. For Participant 139, this is taken even further in their description of a romantic relationship ('like meeting up with [a] lover'). Taken together, the framings within the examples emphasise both the 'pleasure' and the 'comfort' of spending time with these familiar companions. In the context of re-reading, the diachronic and enduring nature of these relationships are also mapped: re-reading is conceptualised as a means of maintaining or developing active and ongoing friendships through time. The re-readers' perception of being able to 'revisit' suggests an understanding of these friends as occupying a stable, physical, and known location.

Further elaborations of this FRIENDS metaphor can be seen in other examples, where participants expressed re-reading in terms of emotional warmth:

[I]f I felt anxious or upset I wil [sic] read a book tgat [sic] feels like a comfy blanket or favourite jumper. (Participant 4)

Sometimes for comfort, it's great to curl up with an old friend (story) on a wet winters [sic] day. (Participant 368)

[W]hy does one wear an old favourite comfy hoodie instead of a new stiff one. (Participant 468)

To stay in their cosy worlds. (Participant 619)

The first example continues the BOOKS ARE FRIENDS metaphor, while the 'wet winters [sic] day' reference suggests their perception of the emotional WARMTH offered by the re-reading experience. The other examples here further conceptually 'blend' (Fauconnier and Turner 2002) domains of experiences. Both CONTAINMENT and WARMTH are suggested in the re-readers' physical and tactile conceptualisations of cosiness, with re-reading construed as a 'comfy blanket', a 'favourite jumper', and a 'cosy', 'comfy hoodie'. Like the re-readers' conceptualisations of their relationships with books as an ongoing friendship, the re-readers construe the comfort offered by these re-reading choices as established and enduring through time: when compared with the more uncomfortable, 'new' and 'stiff' texts, these are 'old', worn and 'comfy' favourites.

4.2.2 RE-READING IS (EMOTIONAL) SUPPORT

The participants who described re-reading as a form of emotional resonance spoke of the books as inciting particular emotions, as in the following examples:

> Because they were book that made a long lasting impression on me. (Participant 375)
>
> If they seemed relevant to my life somehow at the time. (Participant 82)
>
> I think there is a lot of time in the day for a "mood" or "feel" to develop, and sometimes a particular poet comes to mind who seems to match that mood. (Participant 491)
>
> Because I wanted to read something that reflected my emotions. Because reading about happy people makes me happy. (Participant 510)

In these responses, the participants commented that they both chose a text in order to elicit a positively valenced emotion in which they are acted upon by the text ('makes me happy'), or otherwise, or to reflect their existing emotional state ('sometimes a particular poet comes to mind who seems to match that mood') (see Chap. 3). Those re-readers who identified this desire for emotional resonance appreciate 'the reading for sensations it generates' (Doche and Ross 2023, p. 12). Underpinning both motivations is a desire to re-experience particular emotions and a recognition that re-reading offers a means to alter or to enhance an emotional experience.

A prominent sub-code within this category is those who re-read in order to experience nostalgia, in particular, as in the following examples:

> Memory's [sic] of happier reading times. (Participant 54)
>
> Took me back to my childhood. (Participant 159)

[T]o remind me of the person I was when I first read the books, or people I've been when I've re-read the books before. (Participant 510)

Good memories from previous reads. (Participant 524)

The nostalgia is directed towards varied experiences: the participants talk about re-reading as a way to recapture the pleasant experience of reading the text the first time (e.g. 'Good memories from previous reads'), to revisit former versions of themselves (e.g. 'to remind me of the person I was when I first read the books'),[3] or to reminisce on a particular period of their life, such as their childhood. For other re-readers, this nostalgia is directed more specifically to life outside of lockdown, as in the following two examples:

To be fair, just to feel what I felt before. It was like going through a photo album, and you remember that you used to go to the park without thinking of any 2 meters distance, or you used to go to Costa and sit at a table there, or just hug your friends without thinking you will infect them or [sic]. I even read a book about a group of friends in England and when they share a hug near the end, I read that part several times in a row and I started crying because it made me feel as if these stories will be a relic of the past and everything will change in the majority's behaviour towards human interaction. (Participant 219)

Missing reading to my class so rereading their favourites reminds me of reading to them. (Participant 512)

For Participant 512, their desire to re-read is driven by the need to simulate a missed part of their everyday work life before the pandemic. For Participant 219, re-reading for nostalgia is not positively valenced, unlike most of the other examples in the *nostalgia* code. Instead, the re-reading engenders a closer comparison between the reader's isolation in lockdown life and their life pre-pandemic. Even in this early part of the lockdown, the time before is construed as an experience that cannot be resumed and which is already spatiotemporally distanced ('like going through a photo album'; 'a relic of the past'). Both cases, however, are driven by social

---

[3] An additional SPLIT-SELF metaphor (Lakoff 1996) can be observed across the coded themes in the data, where the re-readers frame their reading choices in simultaneous agentive and patient roles. A discussion of this is beyond the scope of the thematic focus in this chapter, though future research on this topic will contribute to ongoing discussions of the relationship between perceptions of divisions of the self and trauma (Emmott 2002).

motivations; to re-experience everyday social encounters that were previously considered routine.

A recurring metaphor that was drawn on by the participants within this *emotional resonance* category was RE-READING IS MEDICINE:

> Because I loved them and they resonated me and could usually make me feel better as stress relief. (Participant 84)

> I find it very soothing. (Participant 225)

> For comfort, I fall in love with the characters and words and it's been a coping mechanism. (Participant 332)

> If I felt stressed or down I might want to re-read a specific book that I knew would make me feel better. (Participant 733)

In many of these framings, and as we observe in Chap. 3, the text is attributed as the agent enacting on the reader as the patient:. Re-reading incites a positive emotional or physiological reaction, both in more schematically physical mappings ('soothing') and in those that relate to mental health more specifically ('stress relief', 'coping mechanism'). In other responses, and as we highlight in Chap. 4, participants talk about re-reading as a type of therapy, in particular. It is conceptualised as a process or instrument which can be administered by re-readers as needed. In all mappings within this metaphor, the ameliorative, restorative, and 'soothing' properties of re-reading are emphasised.

4.3 Changes in Re-reading Since Lockdown

These final sections consider the two most prominent themes the participants drew on in their reflections on re-reading habits since the start of the lockdown:

4.3.1 RE-READING IS A JOURNEY: ESCAPE SCENARIO

If READING IS A JOURNEY, then RE-READING IS A JOURNEY that follows a well-worn path where the destination is already decided. Ministero et al. (2021, p. 10) found that habitual '[r]ereaders were more transportable even when controlling for reading tendencies more generally'. Like the conceptualisations of BOOKS ARE FRIENDS, the re-readers who drew on a JOURNEY metaphor to describe their re-reading in the pandemic framed their reflections in terms of physical visit to a known fictional world.[4]

[I] re-read to re-enter a world I have enjoyed and to reconnect with those characters. (Participant 567)

I like revisiting the alternate realities within their pages (I also mine them for role-playing game plots...) (Participant 579)

I like re reading books which have incredible world-building, because I find it comforting and exciting to re-immerse myself in the world entirely. (Participant 685)

I have vivid imagination and I delve in the book. (Participant 729)

In these examples, the re-readers perceived themselves as the agent and traveller who initiates the process and who are also, emotionally, 'somewhat changed by the journey' (Gerrig and Rapp 2004, p. 267) (e.g. 'I find it comforting and exciting'). Further, the re-readers who drew on this metaphor described their reflections in terms of immersive scenarios, with re-reading offering the opportunity for re-immersion or for 'mining' which align with a GOOD IS DOWN orientational axis of movement.

In Chaps. 3 and 4, we identified the desire for escape and distraction among the participants in relation to their more general reading habits. The participant responses that draw on RE-READING IS A JOURNEY also specifically construe their motivations for re-reading in lockdown as a form of ESCAPE, as an elaboration (Lakoff and Turner 1989; Semino 2008, p. 45) of the JOURNEY metaphor. The re-readers conceptualised their desire to re-read as a physical movement away from the unpleasant here and now (Usherwood and Toyne 2002) and as an act of avoiding emotions brought on by the pandemic (Cho et al. 2021).

---

[4] McLaughlin's (2020) account of re-reading *The Lord of the Rings* during the UK lockdown reflects on the desire to re-read stories that are based on journeys in times of physical restriction. While it is clear to see how stories that feature travel may aid re-readers' desire to experience transportation, it is noteworthy that such stories are used to support mental health in other contexts. The meditation app *Calm*, for example, which has millions of international subscribers, has collections of 'Sleep Stories' thematically categorised under 'Train' and 'Travel' in its virtual library.

[B]ecause it's very comforting to have a familiar read which you know is guaranteed to give you pleasure and take you to another place. (Participant 125)

To take me out of my house. (Participant 142)

Those fantasy storylines are bittersweet and allow me to escape our current situation even for a brief moment. (Participant 284)

To divert from my research and lose myself in historical era. (Participant 404)

Ditto with the Tolkien—lengthy isolation has let me 'disappear' into that world. (Participant 566)

More generally, reading for escape is considered one of the most conscious perceptions of readers (Usherwood and Toyne 2002), offering a form of liberation that can be either physical or cognitive (Garner 2020). While for many, reading is considered a distraction from everyday, monotonous tasks and unpleasant or difficult realities (Usherwood and Toyne 2002; Garner 2020), '[t]o other individuals, reading offers a far more foundational refuge in a great spectrum of difficult situations' (Begum 2011, p. 741). Re-reading as a means of creating a refuge from the pandemic is identified by our participants: they construed it as a way to 'divert' attention from present obstacles and as a movement where the transportation is totalising ('lose myself', 'disappear'). The visiting scenarios mentioned above involve the readers performing the action, and in the ESCAPE scenarios the transport is more extreme movement and often conceptualised with the reader in the role of patient, with re-reading 'guaranteed to [...] take you to another place'.

Participants who conceptualised re-reading in these terms were also found to foreground their current physical location as one of restriction or containment, emphasising their physical confinement at the same time as the experience of liberation offered through re-reading. Like the conceptualisations of BOOKS ARE FRIENDS, the re-readers viewed fictional worlds as a fixed location that endures through time:

I wanted to be in a happy space. (Participant 181)

Revisit favorite characters or worlds, find refuge with comforting books whose plots I already know, whose characters are good people trying to do right by each other. (Participant 255)

To escape to a safe place with characters I know and problems with solutions. (Participant 451)

[I]t's my comfort zone. (Participant 828)

Aligning with the references to comfort and WARMTH explored, the re-readers again draw on a CONTAINMENT image schema (Johnson 1987) in their conceptualisation of ESCAPE. Here, the 'space' or 'zone' is construed as a physical space that envelops the re-reader. Additionally, it is notable that the lexical choices in the manifestations of this metaphor draw on descriptions of this space that otherwise collocate with *war*: 'refuge', 'zone', and 'safe place'. Though not explicitly identified by the participants in these descriptions, the implication is that COVID-19, or the lockdown experience more generally, is understood as an aggressor that incites people to flee. This interpretation is supported by Semino's (2021) research on the war metaphors used to describe COVID-19 metaphors in the early pandemic, where she found that public discourse frequently conceptualised the virus as an enemy to be fought.

4.3.2 Predictability and Known Endings

The final, prominent theme referenced by the re-readers was their desire for predictability and known endings in the early lockdown. The desire to have 'No surprises' (Participant 659) in their reading experiences aligns with our participants' desire to prioritise their mental and emotional health during this time. In wider reading research, prior knowledge of a story, and knowing that characters will be safe or will not change, 'should be calming' (Ministero et al. 2021, p. 3). Seeking a familiar story, albeit one that has been read before or one that follows a formulaic genre template, suggests that the re-readers are emotionally aligning with the characters and their desire for a 'success preference' in the story's solution (Rapp and Gerrig 2005). At the same time, re-reading for predictability can help support readers' belief systems: for example, a preference for returning to romance novels 'may reinforce the belief that such relational dynamics are possible and occur in real life', while re-reading crime fiction will reliably 'offer a world in which safety and order is always restored' (Ministero et al. 2021, p. 9). This latter emphasis on the resolution of a story is similarly foregrounded by the participants, who talked about the importance of knowing 'the outcome' and 'the ending':

Escapism from the initial anxiety that lockdown caused. I knew the outcome and felt safe. (Participant 95)

Very much the same reason: knowing "the ending" to something (and all the unpleasant twists) takes away a lot of anxiety in reading, leaving you to just ... enjoy the story. (Participant 387)

For familiarity, the books I tend to reread are the books I must've reread at least 5 times since owning them. They provide comfort because I can see the twists coming and I know that there is a happy ending awaiting my favourite characters. (Participant 843)

In such descriptions, the re-readers drew together and conflated the metaphors and domains mentioned so far in this chapter. The JOURNEY metaphor is evoked in the re-readers' conceptualisations of the path of the story. Having read the text before, they can see 'the twists coming' and are forewarned against 'unpleasant twists'. Equally, the re-readers showed a concern for the fate of the characters with whom they had developed a relationship (e.g. 'I know that there is a happy ending awaiting my favourite characters'). Again, the texts, and the acts of re-reading, assumed an agentive, caregiving role: it 'takes away a lot of the anxiety' which ultimately provides 'comfort' and makes the re-readers feel 'safe'. These familiar journeys are conceptualised as cognitively easier (e.g. 'it was sometimes easier to go back to a known quantity/non-suspenseful reading experience', Participant 251) and ones that prioritised being able to 'just...enjoy the story'.

5 Conclusion

The participants' reflections reveal a number of motivations that have guided their choices of re-reading in the early pandemic and the experiences of reassurance and emotional support brought about by returning to familiar storylines. The prevailing motivation for comfort and familiarity lends support to the Ministero et al. (2021) observation that people reread to fulfil unmet social needs, and this is further suggested in the BOOKS ARE FRIENDS metaphor whereby re-reading is seen as a way of continuing these relationships through time. Equally, the desire to re-experience particular emotions is perceived as an antidote for the current reality, or in the context of capturing nostalgia or seeking opportunities to reminisce, a means of re-experiencing some of the social elements of pre-lockdown life. While re-reading as a wider reading habit is perceived as a natural preference arising from distinct personality traits, the physical constraints of the lockdown created an external environment which both invited and exacerbated feelings of anxiety and isolation, even among those for whom these traits are not naturally part of their psychological profile.

The key changes identified by the participants between their pre-lockdown re-reading habits and their re-reading preferences since the start of lockdown suggest a prioritisation of re-reading for escape, but also for predictability. In both these thematic codes, the book or the act of re-reading is construed as an enveloping space that either transports re-readers in a totalising, immersive way, or else one that is perceived as a known, secure place of refuge that can be returned to as needed.

References

Andrews, Travis M. 2021. Here's why deep down we like rewatching the same old movies and shows – especially during the pandemic. The Washington Post: https://www.washingtonpost.com/arts-entertainment/2021/02/18/rewatchable-movies-tv-shows/. 21 June 2023.

Begum, Soheli. 2011. Readers' advisory and underestimated roles of escapist reading.

Booth, Wayne C. 1980. 'The way I loved George Eliot': Friendship with books as a neglected critical metaphor. *The Kenyon Review* 2 (2): 4–27.

Boyd, Brian. 2009. *On the origin of stories. Evolution, cognition and fiction*. Cambridge MA and London: The Belknap Press of Harvard University Press.

Bray, Joe. 2007. The 'dual voice' of free indirect discourse: A reading experiment. *Language and Literature* 16 (1): 37–52.

Cho, Hyerim, Wan-Chen Lee, Alex Urban, Li-Min Huang, and Yi Long. 2021. 'I don't want a book that's going to make me sad or stressed out, especially in this day and age': Fiction reading (and healing) in a pandemic. *Proceedings of the Association for Information Science and Technology* 58 (10): 420–424.

Culpeper, Jonathan. 2001. *Language and characterisation: People in plays and other texts*. London: Routledge.

Davies, Ben, Christina Lupton, and Johanne G. Schmidt. 2022. Old books in new times. In *Reading novels during the Covid-19 pandemic*, 72–88. Oxford: Oxford University Press.

Dixon, Peter, Marisa Bortolussi, Leslie C. Twilley, and Alice Leung. 1993. Literary processing and interpretation: Towards empirical foundations. *Poetics* 22 (1): 5–33.

Doche, A., and A.S. Ross. 2023. 'Here is my shameful confession. I don't really "get" poetry': Discerning reader types in responses to Sylvia Plath's *Ariel* on Goodreads. *Textual Practice* 37: 976–996.

Emmott, Catherine. 2002. 'Split-selves' in fiction and in medical 'life-stories': Cognitive linguistic theory and narrative practice. In *Cognitive stylistics: Language and cognition in text analysis*, ed. Elena Semino and Jonathan Culpeper, 153–182. Amsterdam: John Benjamins.

Fauconnier, Gilles, and Mark Turner. 2002. *The way we think: Conceptual blending and the Mind's hidden complexities*. Plymouth: Basic Books.

Garner, Jane. 2020. "Almost like freedom": Prison libraries and reading as facilitators of escape. *Library Quarterly: Information, Community, Policy* 90 (1): 5–19.

Gerrig, Richard. 1993. *Experiencing narrative worlds: On the psychological activities of Reading*. New Haven: Yale University Press.

Hakemulder, Frank. 2007. Tracing foregrounding in responses to film. *Language and Literature* 16 (2): 125–139.

Harrison, Chloe, and Louise Nuttall. 2018. Re-reading in stylistics. *Language and Literature* 27 (3): 176–195.

———. 2019. Cognitive grammar and reconstrual: Re-experiencing Margaret Atwood's 'The freeze-dried groom'. In *Experiencing fictional worlds*, ed. B. Neurohr and E. Stewart-Shaw, 135–154. Amsterdam: Benjamins.

———. 2021. Rereading as retelling: Re-evaluations of perspective in narrative fiction. In *Narrative retellings: Stylistic approaches*, ed. M. Lambrou, 217–234. London: Bloomsbury.

Holland, Norman N. 1988. *The brain of Robert frost*. New York: Routledge.

Ingram, Joanne, and Zoe Luckett. 2019. My friend Harry's a wizard: Predicting parasocial interaction with characters from fiction. *Psychology of Popular Media Culture* 8 (2): 148–158.

Iser, Wolfgang. 1989. *Prospecting: From reader response to literary anthropology*. Baltimore: John Hopkins University Press.

Jeffries, Lesley. 2001. Schema affirmation and white asparagus: Cultural multilingualism among readers of texts. *Language and Literature* 10 (4): 325–343.

Johnson, Mark. 1987. *The body in the mind: The bodily basis of meaning, imagination and reason*. Chicago: Chicago University Press.

Lakoff, George. 1996. Sorry, I'm not myself today: The metaphor system for conceptualizing the self. In *Spaces, worlds and grammars*, ed. Gilles Fauconnier and Eve Sweetser, 91–123. Chicago: University of Chicago Press.

Lakoff, George, and Mark Johnson. 1980. *Metaphors we live by*. Chicago: Chicago University Press.

Lakoff, George, and Mark Turner. 1989. *More than cool reason: A field guide to poetic metaphor*. Chicago: University of Chicago Press.

Langacker, Ronald W. 2008. *Cognitive grammar: A basic introduction*. Oxford: Oxford University Press.

McLaughlin, David. 2020. The road goes ever on and on: Re-reading *the Lord of the rings* in lockdown. *Literary Geographies* 6 (2): 203–207.
Miall, David. 2006. *Literary reading: Empirical and theoretical studies*. Frankfurt am Main: Peter Lang Publishing.
Miall, David, and Don Kuiken. 1994. Foregrounding, defamiliarization, and affect: Response to literary stories. *Poetics* 22 (5): 389–407.
Ministero, Lauren, Melanie C. Green, Shira Gabriel, and Jennifer Valenti. 2021. Back where I belong: Rereading as a risk-free pathway to social connection. *Psychology of Aesthetics, Creativity and the Arts* 16 (1): 97–109.
Musolff, Andreas. 2006. Metaphor scenarios in public discourse. *Metaphor and Symbol* 21 (1): 23–38.
Nuttall, Louise, and Chloe Harrison. 2020. Wolfing down the *twilight* series: Metaphors for reading in online reviews. In *Contemporary media stylistics*, ed. Helen Ringrow and Stephen Pihlaja, 35–59. London: Bloomsbury.
Palmer, Alan. 2004. *Fictional minds*. Nebraska: University of Nebraska Press.
Rapp David, N., and Richard J. Gerrig. 2005. Predilections for narrative outcomes: The impact of story contexts and reader preferences. *Journal of Memory and Language* 54: 54–67.
Rowling Joanne, K. 1997–2007. *The Harry Potter series*. London: Bloomsbury.
Sanford, Anthony J., and Patrick Sturt. 2002. Depth of processing in language comprehension: Not noticing the evidence. *Trends in Cognitive Sciences* 6 (9): 382–386.
Semino, Elena. 2008. *Metaphor in discourse*. Cambridge: Cambridge University Press.
———. 2021. 'Not soldifers but fire-fighters' - Metaphors and Covid-19. *Health Communication* 36 (1): 50–58.
Semino, Elena, Z. Demjén, and J. Demmen. 2016. An integrated approach to metaphor and framing in cognition, discourse and practice, with an application to metaphors for cancer. *Applied Linguistics*: 1–22.
Sillett, Andrew. 2020. *Die Another Day*…and another: Why I've watched the same Bond film every week for six months. *The Telegraph*, Accessed May 16 2023 https://www.telegraph.co.uk/men/the-filter/die-another-day-another-watched-bond-film-every-week-six-months/
Spacks, Patricia M. 2011. *On rereading*. Harvard: Harvard University Press.
Stockwell, Peter. 2009. *Texture: A cognitive aesthetics of Reading*. Edinburgh: Edinburgh University Press.
Usherwood, Bob, and Jackie Toyne. 2002. *Journal of Librarianship and Information Science* 34 (1): 33–41.
Waller, Alison. 2020. *Rereading childhood books: A poetics*. London: Bloomsbury.
Wendell, Sarah. 2020. For a lot of book lovers, rereading old favourites is the only reading they can manage at the moment. *The Washington Post*. https://www.washingtonpost.com/entertainment/books/for-a-lot-of-book-lovers-rereading-old-favorites-is-the-only-reading-they-can-manage-at-the-moment/

2020/05/01/19c3cd4c-8bbe-11ea-ac8a-fe9b8088e101_story.html. Accessed 02 March 2023.

White, Rebecca. 2018. "Let other pens dwell on guilt and misery": Jane Austen and escapism, from trench warfare to YouTube fanvids. *Women's Writing* 25 (4): 486–498.

Xue, Shuwei, Arthur M. Jacobs, and Jana Lüdtke. 2020. What is the difference? Rereading Shakespeare's sonnets – An eye tracking study. *Frontiers in Psychology* 11: 421.

Zunshine, Lisa. 2006. Why we read fiction. In *Theory of mind and the novel*. Columbus: The Ohio State University Press.

CHAPTER 6

Lockdown Experiences of Social Reading

Abstract This chapter examines a number of related issues and findings concerned with the social aspect of reading and how the pandemic may have altered the ways that participants accessed books and discussed their reading with others. We first explore both the personal and social practices of reading, examining what we know about reading in social contexts. We examine how COVID-19 undoubtedly affected the ways in which these practices are conceived and undertaken by readers, highlighting the increased affordances of online tools such as Zoom and MS Teams to set up virtual reading groups. We then turn to our data to consider two specific questions, comparing reported behaviours pre- and during the pandemic: participants' preferred way of reading; and how frequently and in what formats they talked about their reading with others. The chapter thus explores the extent to which participants perceived the pandemic had affected the specific formats and situations in which books were read and or discussed.

Keywords Social reading • Reading culture • Reading groups • Discussing reading

© The Author(s), under exclusive license to Springer Nature Switzerland AG 2024
A. Boucher et al., *Reading Habits in the COVID-19 Pandemic*,
https://doi.org/10.1007/978-3-031-52753-1_6

1 Introduction

In this chapter, we discuss some of the meaningful ways in which participants reported any changes to the situational aspect of reading, and we explore how the pandemic may have altered the ways that participants accessed books and discussed their reading with others. We specifically examine how the pandemic reshaped reading communities and how these communities took shape over lockdown in new, but everyday, social contexts. These observations highlight how readers' experiences and understanding of book spaces, in the sense of both physical and interpersonal reading situations, shifted and evolved across the early lockdown period in response to changes in everyday circumstances, both national and personal.

2 Context

2.1 Solitary and Social Reading

The 'situation' of reading, as we understand it today, is dominated by a series of tropes with a powerful cultural hold. One of the most influential of these tropes is the image of the serious and scholarly (almost always male) solitary reader, the representative power of this image finding its roots in a long tradition of Christian art stretching from the Medieval age to well into the nineteenth century (Long 2003). The single, solitary scholar who is 'withdrawn from the world and suspended from human community and action' (Long 2003, p. 2) finds his heirs in all those modern readers who aspire to be 'serious' readers (2003, p. 3). The sheer number of these heirs still in existence is evidenced by the extreme reactions to the kind of 'frivolous' reading encompassed by what Fuller and Rehberg Sedo (2015) call, 'mass reading events' (MREs). The Richard and Judy Book Club is a prime example of a mass reading event in the UK. In the original format of the club, TV hosts Richard and Judy chose a weekly book and interviewed the author on their chat show. Since 2009, the club has continued online on a website run with book retailer W.H.Smith and via various social media platforms. Bloom, among others, finds these kind of shared reading programmes repugnant, comparing what he calls 'mass reading bees' to the idea that 'we are all going to pop out and eat Chicken McNuggets or something else horrid at once' (cited in Kirkpatrick 2002). Similarly, O'Hagan brands 'Richard and Judy culture' as a 'coarsening' of literary culture in the UK, claiming that the books that the television presenters choose 'oversell a reduced, unimaginative notion of what literary enjoyment might be' (cited in Boztas 2008). Bloom and O'Hagan's views, that the municipal organisation involved in MREs somehow cheapens the personal and private experience of reading, are testament to the enduring hold of the solitary reader trope, throwing cold water on Collins' (2002, p. 18) prematurely exuberant conclusion that the rise of shared reading en masse, such as taking part in Richard and Judy's Book Club, has contributed to a democratisation of 'what counts as a quality reading experience'. In fact, Price (2019) has posited that any suggestion that our culture is shifting away from the concept of the studious solitary reader of long-form fiction as our 'ideal reader' normally engenders a moral panic. The potential loss of this image from our shared iconography of reading therefore tops the list of twenty-first century anxieties about reading habits.

The long-standing dominance of this particular image of reading can also, inevitably, lead to difficulties for those wanting to research the whole gamut of contemporary reading practices. Scholarly focus on the moment of isolation, highlighted by the culturally powerful concept of the solitary reader, has enabled the construction of a hierarchy of reading in which the reader is imagined as coming after, and hence being subordinate to, the writer, who is consequently prioritised as a source of meaning (Radway 2001). The existence of such a hierarchy has stunted the appetite for research into social reading as a phenomenon from which readers draw meaning and significance and hindered academic investigation of those who share their reading experiences within the context of book groups.

This situation has not been helped by the fact that the dominant image of serious and solitary reading and its more 'frivolous' counterpart, social reading, have been held in a perpetual tension constructed on gender lines, whereby the former is associated with men, the latter with women (Long 2003). The continued existence of this gendered dichotomy has meant that research into specific examples of social reading, the attempt to get behind sales statistics (Davies et al. 2022, p. 3) and 'peer into ... [the] hearts' (Price 2019, p. 50) of readers in the very act of reading and discussing books, has fallen historically to feminist researchers such as Long (2003), Radway (1991), and Sweeney (2010). These researchers depict reading groups and sharing 'book talk', not as superficial light entertainment, but as an opportunity for individuals to negotiate with the social conditions of their lives and the contemporary historical moment through which they are living (Long 2003, p. 21). Such an understanding demonstrates how shared reading is both a social process and a social formation (Rehberg Sedo 2011b, p. 1). In contrast to the solitary reader trope, this model of reading highlights the inherent sociability of books (Price 2019), the fact that they are written in a language 'whose very grammars, genres, and figures of speech encode collectivity' (Long 2003, p. 2). It is to this conception of language to which the author Raymond Williams (1978/2010) attests when he discusses his awareness when writing of both a society and a language which seem larger than himself as a solitary writer. He thus seems to suggest that writers compose with an interactive audience already in mind, hinting that books can be seen as 'social' from the very moment of their inception.

2.2 Uncovering Reading 2.0

The data generated in our project has enabled an investigation into social reading that focuses both on participants' experiences of sharing reading online, and on instances of social reading with family, friends, and colleagues in a variety of different settings. Our analysis in this chapter explores the shifting dynamics of these social reading practices and examines the redirection of reading activities to social spaces that are engendered both physically and virtually. Consequently, the discussion contributes to burgeoning research on social reading as a phenomenon.

Notoriously a diffuse, interdisciplinary field, research on the history of books and their readers has historically drawn on a wide range of different disciplines, from bibliography to ethnography, from material book history to cultural and media studies, all of which come accompanied by their own specific methodologies. Studies on the phenomenon of social reading from a more literary perspective are still fairly limited. The edited collection by Rehberg Sedo (2011a) is one exception, including historical essays by Schellenberg Betty (2011) on an epistolary community of Bluestockings in the eighteenth century and Hartley (2011) on nineteenth-century reading groups in Britain. In contrast, contemporary research in stylistics observes a movement towards accounts of social readings through different perspectives. For example, there is an established tradition of stylistic studies drawing on reading group discussions—either through the observation of discussions that take place within existing reading groups or in the simulation of reading group discussions through focus groups—as a form of contextualised social reader data, enabling researchers to explore interpersonal dynamics within reading groups and the social negotiation of booktalk (Peplow 2016; Canning 2017; Mason 2019; Whiteley and Peplow 2020; Giovanelli 2022) or as an indirect measure of accessing interactive discussions of emotional experiences of reading (e.g. Whiteley 2011). In other less socioculturally focused stylistic projects, interactive reader response data is drawn on as a way of contextualising processes of reading, offering a means of exploring the relationship between reading and cognition (e.g. Norledge 2019; Harrison forthcoming).

In addition to this research on social reading in face-to-face contexts, contemporary research on social reading also explores virtual contexts such as Zoom, Microsoft Teams, or Google Meet (Rehberg Sedo 2011c). The use of social media sites by book lovers to communicate their reading has also created a range of source material for those researchers exploring book and reading history through the framework of applied linguistics. Such research explores communities that form through book lovers' shared usage of social media platforms such as Goodreads, Instagram (#Bookstagram), TikTok (#BookTok), YouTube (BookTube), and other online literary forums (see, e.g., Thomas and Round 2016; Vlieghe et al. 2016; Harrison and Nuttall 2020; Roig-Vila et al. 2021). Roig-Vila et al. (2021, pp. 1–2) suggest that twenty-first-century BookTubers promote 'a new form of social reading [...] as a positive habit', with their online content contributing to an understanding of reading that has been 'socialized and transformed into a constant conversation'. Vlieghe et al. (2016) further suggest that in hosting this kind of continuous conversation, social media sites function as 'affinity spaces', gathering together like-minded people in one (online) place. The data available online and from within these affinity spaces have enabled linguists to investigate social reading from the perspective of *how* readers represent themselves and their reading experiences and how they negotiate their relationships with other readers within online discourse communities (Peplow et al. 2016; Harrison and Nuttall 2020).

It is clear how the availability of data preserved on social media sites has opened up research on everyday instances of social reading in a way that was impossible before the Internet provided a forum for vast quantities of people across the world to converse about their shared interests. Insight into everyday examples of shared reading in the past (as opposed to that taking place within more formally arranged groups) can now be garnered predominantly from the domestic vignettes included in more general overviews of reading. It is thus we find out about the cloth merchant who recalled in his 1756 diary how he did his accounts while his wife read

Richardson's *Clarissa* to him (Tadmor 1996, p. 165) and hear reports of the various evenings the Austen family spent reading as a form of everyday family entertainment, listening to each other read contemporary authors of the day, such as Cowper, Southey, Scott, and (Charlotte) Lennox (described in Manguel 1996, p. 122).

Beyond the new 'spaces' offered by the Internet, very little attention has been paid to the way that reading as a social practice exists in the ether of a 'reading culture' (Griswold 2008). Few studies take into account the small acts of reading or discussion of reading that occur as part of our social infrastructure (e.g. socialisation into reading, supportive talk about reading, and the designation of cultural value) that allow a reading culture to develop in much the same way as the infrastructure of modern transportation, comprising roads, airports, and refuelling opportunities, allows us to be globally mobile (Long 2003, pp. 9–11). This is the kind of developing reading culture, 'reading 2.0', that savvy librarians seek to harness when they explore the way that reading can be 'transformed from that quiet room into an exciting, relevant twenty-first century social experience' (D'Andrea 2010). However, while we, along with those canny librarians, might sense the existence of a more social 2.0 version of reading that fully harnesses new and evolving technological affordances, few researchers have so far attempted to find any concrete evidence for the contemporary versions of everyday domestic conversations of the kind enjoyed by the Richardson fan (Tadmor 1996) and the Austen family (Manguel 1996). The data from this study provides a way of exploring these experiences within the unique context of the emergency lockdown in 2020.

3 Methodology

The data in this chapter are drawn from a series of sub-questions that formed Questions 9 and 10 in the *Aston Lockdown Reading Survey Corpus*:

9. Before lockdown, did you typically discuss your reading experiences with others?
9.a. If yes, in what kinds of contexts did you discuss your reading experiences (please select all that apply):

   face to face (in person)
   face to face (video platform)
   over the phone
   social media

online review sites
other

9.b. Before the lockdown, how frequently did you discuss your reading experience with others?

more than once a week
about once a week
about once every couple of weeks
about once every month
about once every couple of months
other

10. Since the start of the lockdown, have you discussed your reading experiences with others?

10.a. If yes, in what kinds of contexts have you discussed your experiences (please select all that apply):

face to face (in person)
face to face (video platform)
over the phone
social media
online review sites
other

10.b. Since the start of the lockdown, how frequently have you discussed your reading experiences with others?

more than once a week
about once a week
about once every couple of weeks
about once every month
about once every couple of months
other

In our analysis section, we discuss sub-corpora consisting of free-text responses amounting to a total of 7204 tokens. These responses were inductively coded, identifying relevant themes through a recursive procedure, moving backwards and forwards between existing research consulted for the literature review and an initial overview of the free-text responses in the survey.

4 Analysis

4.1 Making Connections: On, Over, or Via Zoom

Given the fact that the history of books consistently interlocks with the history of social and technological change (Price 2019), it is unsurprising that during lockdown, readers harnessed available technology to move their discussions about books, both formal and informal, online, with our data showing that the number of people using video-call software increased dramatically from 20.8% before the pandemic to 67.4% during the pandemic. Of those participants who chose to use the free-text box in response to the questions about their use of video calls to talk about books during the pandemic, 38% mentioned Zoom by name, with the next most popular video-calling software, Skype and Microsoft Teams, both being mentioned by 5% of respondents.

Looking specifically at those respondents who chose to utilise the free-text boxes, we can see that only three people mentioned that their book club was conducted online pre-pandemic, rising to 36 during the first lockdown period. These findings, and those above, regarding video-calling software, are consistent with BookBrowse (2020) study on how book clubs, predominantly in the US and Canada, functioned during lockdown. The headline statistics in this report are that 65% of book clubs still meeting during lockdown were doing so virtually, almost all of these groups using Zoom. For the compilers of the BookBrowse report, this is evidence of the enduring strength of community during times of hardship, which has here been cemented by a love of books.

The responses of those participants who mention Zoom by name (in their answers to the question related to the use of video-call software or in their answers to later questions) capture a moment in time in which differences in linguistic usage highlight changes in reading culture. One of the many differences in the way that respondents referred to Zoom, or alternatives such as Skype or Microsoft Teams, was in their varying uses of prepositions. Ten of the participants who mentioned video-calling software used the preposition 'via', such as Participant 20 who mentioned 'Bookclub meetings via Zoom' and Participant 833 who similarly commented that their book club was 'now via video call'. The use of 'via' as a preposition to indicate the use of video technology foregrounds its utilitarian value as a tool for communication. However, other participants, who used prepositions such as 'on' or 'onto' or even 'over', for example, 'we pick a book each week in turn to discuss over Facetime' (Participant 111) or 'with friends on Zoom chats' (Participant 615), indicated that they viewed the video technology as providing almost a literal rather than a metaphorical platform on which to meet, or alternatively, that they viewed the use of relatively new software such as Zoom and Facetime as the equivalent of talking over the phone. The same sense of embodiment, as suggested by the use of the preposition 'on', is also indicated by participants' references to Zoom as an alternative physical location for their book club meetings, as in Participant 639's report that 'we have moved the previously mentioned pub book club to zoom'.

As a collective, the participants in this survey did not seem to be sure of the status that Zoom, and other software enabling video calls, had in their lives and did not yet completely comprehend its rules of operation as a form of communication. Another example of this hesitancy is indicated by the fact that the word 'Zoom' functions as part of a variety of different word classes in participants' responses. It is often used as a head noun, for example, in the response 'with a work colleague over Zoom' (Participant 714); as a noun modifier, as in 'Zoom discussion' (Participant 494) or even, on occasion, as a verb, such as 'Zoom with my book group' (Participant 109), with the pronoun 'I' elided. Used as noun modifier, often seen pre-modifying the plural noun 'meetings' (e.g. by Participant 245, 274, 663, and 826), it could be argued that 'Zoom' in this sense is one example of the explosion of neologisms generated during the pandemic.[1]

Collectively, the responses to this survey bear witness to how rapidly our language changed during the period of lockdown, with new words and phrases formed as 'a coping mechanism to articulate [...] new experiences and responses to the unprecedented events brought about by the pandemic' (Pura et al. 2022, p. 95). These linguistic changes, in turn, are evidence of cultural shifts in our experience of reading. As Price (2019, p. 23) argues, 'far from providing a refuge from history, books make history – not just through the ideas they vehicle, but also through the technologies created for manufacturing and distributing them', to which we can now include the software utilised for sharing our thoughts on them. Our data reveal that, during the first lockdown, people found a way to preserve the inherent interactivity of books, trialling new technology in

---

[1] The most common mechanism by which this kind of language change occurred during the pandemic was via compounding; see Pura et al. (2022).

order to keep up their discussions and employing linguistic dexterity as they tried out new ways to articulate what they were doing.

4.2 Finding New Spaces for Social Reading

The data generated as part of this project provide a glimpse into a shared life of books that had been at least partially curtailed by lockdown restrictions. As we highlight in the previous section, many people adapted quickly to the situation and found alternative ways to engage in reading, but this does not conceal the sense of loss felt by many participants, as indicated by their frequent use of adverbs in responses. Asked about the face-to-face conversations that they had during lockdown, participants frequently drew attention to changes in their routines regarding with whom they discussed their reading:

> only with my household. (Participant 162)
>
> only with family at home. (Participant 269)
>
> only with housemates. (Participant 339)
>
> just my husband. (Participant 421)

There is a sense here of readers' awareness of a thriving 'reading culture' (Griswold 2008) that has just been diminished. The readers' responses suggest their understanding of a restriction of a wider community of readers, their social reading networks suddenly confined to those in their physical vicinity.

Participants also frequently mentioned the 'bubbles' they had formed during lockdown, and discussing reading clearly become a part of these close-knit communities. For example, Participant 75 commented that she had discussed books 'recently, since forming a bubble' and talking of her mother, Participant 408 reported that 'I discussed with her after we were able to make a bubble of our households'. The word 'bubble' was used before 2020 to refer to a situation of insularity, but with negative connotations, for example, to describe a 'political bubble' or an 'ideological bubble' to metaphorically refer to a dangerous inflexibility of ideas. During the COVID-19 crisis, the term 'bubble' became repurposed to refer, in a positive sense, to close contact between a small group of family or friends, who were nevertheless still isolated from the general public at large (Herwick Edgar 2021). The discussion of reading within one's 'bubble' thus extends its inherent suggestion of intimacy and closeness.

Our data also highlight glimpses of vignettes that suggest that without access to many traditional forms of entertainment, extended families in 'bubbles' spent more time reading, and talking about reading, together. Participant 144 reported that they discussed books 'over meals with my wife', and this was the same for Participants 70 and 677. Participant 260 wrote at more length than many participants and commented that

> I suppose face-to-face discussions with family and my partner increased within lockdown as I spent longer periods of time in the day discussing what I was reading due to a lack of other entertainment taking up conversations.

Other similar responses included:

> I have started reading to my son again (who is 12 years old—surprisingly, he loves it—I thought he was too old. (Participant 255)

> I also talk to my kids about what we're all reading. (Participant 175)

> My little sister reads a lot so I've started discussing these things with her. (Participant 424)

There is a suggestion here that many participants had rediscovered the pleasures of domestic reading reminiscent of that described in scenes from earlier centuries (Manguel 1996; Tadmor 1996).

Generally speaking, this increased appreciation of the domestic setting as a context for social reading was reported as coming about as the result of a conscious choice made by each participant. Respondents reported their decision 'to chat', 'to share', and 'to discuss' in simple sentences combining a personal pronoun and a verb, in the active voice. Participant 355, for example, wrote that 'I have discussed books more with my children', Participant 367 commented that 'I talk to my wife about what I'm reading more', and Participant 408 stated 'my mum and I share a lot of our books'. It is interesting, therefore, to note instances when respondents used passive constructions to discuss the events of lockdown, and/or removed their own agency from the sentences they use to report this (see also Chaps. 3 and 5 for further discussions of agency). Participant 260's suggestion that 'I suppose face-to-face discussions with my family and my partner increased within lockdown' and Participant 275's report that 'once lockdown was eased a bit [reading] became part of the conversation in friends (sic) gardens' seem to demonstrate that social reading has a life of its own, above and beyond those who participate in it. This might be further evidence that, given the fact that reading seems to have an almost physical existence, these respondents see themselves belonging to a reading class, if not a reading culture (Griswold 2008).

Space has always been important in the study of reading communities (Rehberg Sedo 2011b) and what is notable about the spaces mentioned in the data received for this project is the sense that the later part of the lockdown period marked, what could be viewed as a partial physical re-emergence into the world. For example, Participant 275 recalled 'conversation[s] in friends (sic) gardens'; Participant 321 mentioned 'really long walks' with a friend; Participant 485 remembered 'meet[ing] friends in parks'; Participant 811 recounted sharing books 'with neighbours'; and Participant 368 referred to recommending titles to the 'man at corner shop'. From its position at the heart of households and 'bubbles', social reading clearly moved into a transitional semi-public space famously a key stage in the emergence of the public sphere during the Enlightenment period, as traced by Habermas (1991). Given the notorious exclusion of particular individuals from the public sphere, along the lines of race, gender, and even age (Charles and Fuentes-Rohwer 2015; Kulynych 2001; Polletta and Chen 2013), it is tempting to see the semi-public discussions on books that occurred in parks and gardens and with neighbours as the world re-opened, as evidence of a brief moment of utopian social levelling, in which inter-generational, intra-communal contact brought people together through their shared loved of reading.

What is also noteworthy about the semi-public spaces mentioned by name by respondents is that they are outside and therefore part of the natural world. Research has been undertaken on how the pandemic changed our relationship with nature (see, e.g., Office for National Statistics 2021) and Davies et al. (2022) devote an entire chapter of their book on novel reading in the pandemic to reading outdoors. Kuzmičová (2016, p. 18) suggests that the location in which one reads might be linked to our experience of reading through a form of pleasure transfer, in which, for example, the enjoyment of reading in a garden reinforces one's delight in the book being read, and vice versa. While Kuzmičová (2016) is focused on reading rather than the discussion of reading, in their research on the functioning of book clubs during the pandemic, Book Browse (2020, p. 20) also concluded that members enjoyed meeting to talk about books outside.

Although respondents did not make many comments on their experiences of social reading in outdoor spaces, aside from stating that this is what they were doing, there is perhaps the potential for further research here. Throughout their report, Book Browse (2020) certainly suggest that the behaviour of a book club and members' experience of being part of such a group differs according to whether the group meets in a public space such as a library or a private space like the home. Those groups meeting in public places typically spend less time socialising at their book club meeting, compared to those meeting in private spaces. According to BookBrowse (2020, pp. 30–31) meeting virtually has also started to affect the behaviour of book groups, with 20% of groups surveyed reporting that their discussions have been longer since they have been meeting virtually and some commenting that they felt group discussions were more inclusive when they were held online. Such suggestions could clearly be developed through further research: given the long-standing interest on the part of those who research reading communities in different kinds of spaces, it would be valuable to find out more about what influence different contexts, such as the domestic, the semi-public, the formal, and now even the online environment, might have on the way people discuss books in post-lockdown life.

4.3 Social Reading in the Pandemic: We Did It Our Way

Looking across the responses to all the different questions about social reading, there is much evidence that reading generally was used, as we highlighted in Chap. 3, to pass the time. Appropriately, as respondents explored new avenues for filling this time, the verb 'joined' was used eight times in the free-text responses, for example:

[J]oined two groups [...] one focused on Shakespeare, the other on books. (Participant 28)

I have [...] joined a number of cooking groups centred around books. (Participant 375)

I joined a bunch of book groups on Facebook. (Participant 630)

The verb 'started' was used even more frequently and was found ten times in the data, for example:

I started a readalong with my daughter's class. (Participant 5)

[W]e have started an email book club where staff recommend books to each other. (Participant 92)

[W]e also started reading the same books together. (Participant 852)

The adjective 'new' also appears four times, as in

[H]ave just starting trying (sic) Storygraph, a new website. (Participant 158)

[A] new book club set up in lockdown! (Participant 245)

[G]roup server on Discord for new book club. (Participant 510)

Two of these three examples also feature the names of 'new' technological tools that the respondents had incorporated into their lives. Participants often felt as if they had been inaugurated into new communities, such as Participant 638, who claimed to be 'Part of Popsugar [POPSUGAR][2] challenge on FB'. This was even more pronounced for those respondents mentioning new reading matter and new connections linked to the issue of racism, presumably inspired by the Black Lives Matter movement. Participant 435 explained that 'My friends and I have been reading a couple of books to do with black history and how white westerners have affected black and poc throughout the years'. Participant 631 mentioned 'antiracist reading groups', and Participant 638 (of the POPSUGAR reference) a 'FB reading group called Readers Against Racism'.

There is a palpable sense here of participants finding new interests (Shakespeare, cookery books, black history/the history of racism), taking on new challenges (the website Storygraph hosts a range of book-related 'challenges' that you can sign yourself up for as does the POPSUGAR page on Facebook, mentioned by a number of respondents), and connecting with people in new ways (joining book groups on Facebook, conducting a book club via email, initiating readalongs, setting up new servers on Discord). That these new experiences were often undertaken enthusiastically is indicated by the jubilant exclamation mark in the comment made by Participant 245: 'a new book club set up in lockdown!'

Our data also demonstrate that participants used their social media accounts as a way of maintaining a record of how they had spent their time,[3] often making it clear that the way that they had been using these

---

[2] The POPSUGAR reading challenge offers readers a set of prompts to encourage them to read new book. In 2020, readers were given forty standard and ten advanced prompts 'challenging' them, for example, to 'Read a book with a great first line' and 'Read a book on a subject you know nothing about'; see Block (2019).

[3] See also Davies et al. (2022, p. 35) for discussion.

accounts to record, promote, and share their reading had changed significantly during lockdown. This corresponds with the quantitative data generated by the survey, which shows that the use of social media accounts to discuss reading during the lockdown rose by 4%, when compared to usage before the pandemic (from 68.6% to 72.6%). We therefore find multiple examples of this increased usage in the free-text responses:

> I have been leaving more reviews and comments on my goodreads account. (Participant 212)
>
> I posted a picture of me once I'd finished my first lockdown novel. (Participant 693)
>
> I did a book post on ten books I enjoyed reading on Facebook. I am generally a lurker/passive user so that was kind of exceptional for me. (Participant 764)

Clearly exceptional circumstances called for 'exceptional' behaviour, and there is a clear sense here that participants were recording their reading so that they could, as Davies et al. (2022, p. 36) suggest, 'look back on it from a future moment [...] an imaginative proleptic leap from the present into the future in order to make an analeptic return to the present-as-past'.

This sense of dynamic record making is partially evoked by the consistent use of the active voice throughout the comments above, and others like them. The data highlight examples where the reader is the source of control:

> I *posted*. (Participant 693)
>
> I *did*. (Participant 764)
>
> I *created*. (Participant 56)
>
> I *use*. (Participant 270)
>
> I *joined*. (Participant 630)

For these participants, sharing their reading experiences, and connecting with others over these experiences, was a distinct choice and a way of marking time throughout the lockdown period that offered some sense of personal control in the face of global catastrophe.

What is conveyed most strongly in these accounts of posting, joining, using, creating, and doing is the sense of participants finding personal solutions to a very challenging situation. However, regardless of the trends and themes that can clearly be drawn from the data, there were participants who responded to this survey, who reacted to the lockdown situation in a way that could be seen as different or unexpected. While many respondents, as suggested above, reported increased use of their social media accounts to record and share their reading, some even setting up new accounts to do so ('now have a booky Instagram account', Participant 4), there were equally some who reported reduced usage of their social media accounts to discuss books, with a few even declaring that they had stopped using social media altogether. Participant 419 stated, for example, 'I haven't bothered with good reads during lockdown as avoiding spending too much time at a screen', while Participant 485 claimed that 'I've reduced my twitter use to control my access to news'. Participant 355 suggested, more dramatically, that 'I have left social media during the pandemic', and Participant 471 provided a potential reason for this kind of decision, stating that 'I stopped using Instagram recently because it was making me miserable'.

There was also a contrast in the data between those participants who suggest that their intellectual world expanded during the lockdown, finding new interests such as Shakespeare, cookery, or engaging in discourses of anti-racism, and those respondents who suggest that their world was imploding. Participant 188 indicated, sadly, that he discussed reading with his partner less often because she was badly depressed and therefore, they hardly ever saw each other. An equally negative situation was reported by Participant 579, who claimed to have left Twitter 'due to harassment and abuse'. A similar sense of discrepancy can be found between those who felt it important to share their reading experiences during the lockdown, perhaps seeing this almost as a duty, and those who, for their own reasons, tried to avoid this. Participant 685 felt compelled to share a relevant book or passage from a book when they felt that it would be interesting or helpful to a particular friend or an acquaintance. In complete contrast, Participant 111, who had before lockdown been a regular poster on Instagram, found that they were posting less during lockdown because 'of how much my reading increased and didn't want to show off'. They also felt that 'it would not be encouraging to my friends who may not be in a similar situation where they can read and might not be able to concentrate'.

Participant 111 sums up the proviso to all these conclusions that have so far been drawn from this data, perfectly. People lived through so many unique contexts during the pandemic, that although there is clearly evidence to support the fact that the experience of lockdown brought us, in the words of sociologist Sherry Turkle (2017), 'alone together', this developing trope of pandemic reading is ultimately as misconceived as previous tropes, such as our fixation on the solitary novel reader as an ideal that we have somehow lost due to the advancements of the digital revolution. Putting all our faith in one particular iconic image of a reader anaesthetises us against the historical realities of people's reading lives, and once again, as we have highlighted in previous chapters, it is difficult to generalise. Engaging with the practices of social reading means listening carefully to unique experiences; the book is not a bunker, as Price (2019, p. 12) warns us (cf. Chap. 6 on *war* lexis in discourses of re-reading).

5   Conclusion

Our data draw attention to the messy and inconsistent nature of real reading experiences (Auyong 2020, p. 94), particularly exacerbated at a time of global catastrophe and turmoil. The responses provide a series of snapshots of experiences, and conceptualisations, of social reading during this period and suggest that, during lockdown, 'reading' refused to exist simply as an isolated gerund referring to a specific act 'occurring when, and only when, an individual's eyes peruse a text' (Pawley 2002, p. 157). Interpretations of 'reading' during this time cannot be limited to solitary eyes perusing a page and instead must broaden to encompass its social dimensions; as a practice that can be, and was, discussed amongst small and larger communities on video calls, blogs, websites, and a huge array of different social media apps. This incorporation of twenty-first-century technology into the act of reading is a reminder that, as Price (2019, p. 24) eloquently argues, books have always been at the forefront of technological change. They have also, as Price (2019) repeatedly demonstrates, always been an inherently social form. Analysis of our data indicates that considering in detail the impact that different spaces, contexts, and locations might have on social reading would be a fruitful area for burgeoning research on this phenomenon, outlining our changing relationships with books in post-lockdown life. Finally, we have highlighted how the practice of reading was inevitably entangled with the individual circumstances through which people experienced the emergency lockdown of 2020. The responses in our data provide many examples of the kinds of language that people chose to represent their new and shifting experiences of the social elements of reading during this time, revealing insights into reader conceptualisations of book spaces, interpersonal practices, and their re-emergence into the social world.

References

Auyong, Elaine. 2020. What we mean by reading. *New Literary History* 5: 93–114.
Block, Tara. 2019. Find a Cosy Nook, Book-Lovers—the 2020 POPSUGAR Reading Challenge Is Here! https://www.popsugar.co.uk/entertainment/reading-challenge-2020-46911508#photo-46911603. Accessed 10th February 2024.
BookBrowse. 2020. *Book clubs in lockdown*. Saratoga, CA: BookBrowse LLC.
Boztas, Senay. 2008. Richard and Judy 'treat their readers as stupid'. *The Guardian*, August 17.
Canning, Patricia. 2017. Text world theory and real world readers: From literature to life in a Belfast prison. *Language and Literature* 26 (2): 172–187.
Charles, Guy-Uriel, and Luis Fuentes-Rohwer. 2015. Habermas, the public sphere and the creation of a racial counterpublic. *Michigan Journal of Race and Law*. https://doi.org/10.36643/mjrl.21.1.habermas.
Collins, Jim. 2002. High-pop: An introduction. In *High-pop: Making culture into popular entertainment*, ed. Jim Collins, 1–31. Oxford: Blackwell Publishers.
D'Andrea, Debra. 2010. Reading 2.0: From solitary to social. *School Librarian's Workshop* 31: 11–12.
Davies, Ben, Christina Lupton, and Johanne Gormsen Schmidt. 2022. *Reading novels during the Covid-19 pandemic*. Oxford: Oxford University Press.
Fuller, Danielle, and DeNel Rehberg Sedo. 2015. *Reading beyond the book: The practices of contemporary literary culture*. London: Routledge.
Giovanelli, Marcello. 2022. Reading the lockdown: Responding to covid poetry. *Journal of Poetry Therapy* 36: 210–225.
Griswold, Wendy. 2008. *Regionalism and the reading class*. Chicago: University of Chicago Press.
Habermas, Jürgen. 1991. *The structural transformation of the public sphere: An inquiry into a category of bourgeois society*. Trans. T. Burger. Cambridge, Mass: The MIT Press.
Harrison, Chloe. Forthcoming. *The language of Margaret Atwood*. London: Palgrave Macmillan.
Harrison, Chloe, and Louise Nuttall. 2020. Wolfing down the *Twilight* series: Metaphors for reading in online reviews. In *Contemporary media stylistics*, ed. Helen Ringrow and Stephen Pihlaja, 35–59. New York: Bloomsbury Academic.
Hartley, Jenny. 2011. Nineteenth-century reading groups in Britain and the community of the text: An experiment with *little Dorrit*. In *Reading communities from salons to cyberspace*, ed. DeNel Rehberg Sedo, 44–59. Basingstoke: Palgrave Macmillan.
Herwick Edgar, B. 2021. The pandemic has transformed the English language. *GBH News: The Curiosity Desk*, March 9.
Kirkpatrick, David D. 2002. Want a fight? Pick one book for all New Yorkers. *The New York Times*, February 19.

Kulynych, Jessica. 2001. No playing in the public sphere: Democratic theory and the exclusion of children. *Social Theory and Practice* 27: 231–264.
Kuzmičová, Anezka. 2016. Does it matter where you read? Situating narrative in physical environment. *Communication Theory* 26: 290–308.
Long, Elizabeth. 2003. *Book clubs: Women and the uses of reading in everyday life.* Chicago: University of Chicago Press.
Manguel, Albert. 1996. *A history of reading.* London: Flamingo.
Mason, Jessica. 2019. *Intertextuality in practice.* Amsterdam: John Benjamins.
Norledge, Jessica. 2019. Immersive reading and the unnatural text-worlds of 'dead fish'. In *Experiencing fictional worlds,* ed. Ben Neurohr and Lizzie Stewart-Shaw, 157–175. Amsterdam: John Benjamins.
Office for National Statistics. 2021. How has lockdown changed our relationship with nature? *Census 2021.* https://www.ons.gov.uk/economy/environmentalaccounts/articles/howhaslockdownchangedourrelationshipwithnature/2021-04-26. Accessed 16 June 2023.
Pawley, Christine. 2002. 'Seeking significance': Actual readers, specific reading communities. *Book History* 5: 143–160.
Peplow, David. 2016. *Talk about books: A study of reading groups.* London: Bloomsbury.
Peplow, David, Joan Swann, Paolo Trimarco, and Sara Whiteley. 2016. *The discourse of reading groups: Integrating cognitive and sociocultural perspectives.* London: Routledge.
Polletta, Francesca, and Pang Ching Bobby Chen. 2013. Gender and public talk: Accounting for women's variable participation in the public sphere. *Sociological Theory* 31: 291–317.
Price, Leah. 2019. *What do we talk about when we talk about books: The history and future of reading.* New York: Basic Books.
Pura, Cielo May, Leah Gustilo, and Thomas Biermeier. 2022. How the pandemic fuels linguistic change: Lexical innovations in L1 and L2 English varieties. *GEMA Online: Journal of Language Studies* 22: 80–109.
Radway, Janice. 1991. *Reading the romance: Women, patriarchy, and popular literature.* 2nd ed. Chapel Hill: University of North Carolina Press.
———. 2001. Readers and their romances: From literary theory to cultural studies. In *Reception study: From literary theory to cultural studies,* ed. James L. Machor and Philip Goldstein, 213–245. London: Routledge.
Rehberg Sedo, DeNel. 2011a. *Reading communities from salons to cyberspace.* Basingstoke: Palgrave Macmillan.
———. 2011b. Introduction to reading communities: Processes and formations. In *Reading communities from salons to cyberspace,* ed. DeNel Rehberg Sedo, 1–24. Basingstoke: Palgrave Macmillan.
———. 2011c. 'I used to read everything that caught my eye, but…': Cultural authority and intermediaries in a virtual young adult book club. In *Reading communities from salons to cyberspace,* ed. DeNel Rehberg Sedo, 101–122. Basingstoke: Palgrave Macmillan.

Roig-Vila, Rosabel, Héctor Romero-Guerra, and José Rovira-Collado. 2021. BookTubers as multimodal reading influencers: An analysis of subscriber interactions. *Multimodal Technologies and Interaction* 5. https://doi.org/10.3390/mti5070039.

Schellenberg Betty, A. 2011. Reading in an epistolary community in eighteenth-century England. In *Reading communities from salons to cyberspace*, ed. DeNel Rehberg Sedo, 25–43. Basingstoke: Palgrave Macmillan.

Sweeney, Megan. 2010. *Reading is my window: Books and the art of reading in women's prisons*. Chapel Hill: University of North Carolina Press.

Tadmor, Naomi. 1996. 'In the even' my wife read to me': Women, reading and household life in the eighteenth century. In *The practice and representation of Reading in England*, ed. James Raven, Helen Small, and Naomi Tadmor, 162–174. Cambridge: Cambridge University Press.

Thomas, Bronwen, and Julia Round. 2016. Moderating reading and readers online. *Language and Literature: International Journal of Stylistics* 25 (3): 239–253.

Turkle, Sherry. 2017. *Alone together*. 3rd ed. New York: Basic Books.

Vlieghe, Joachim, Jaël Muls, and Kris Rutten. 2016. Everybody reads: Reader engagement with literature in social media environments. *Poetics* 54: 25–37.

Whiteley, Sara. 2011. Talking about 'an accommodation': The implications of discussion group data for community engagement and pedagogy. *Language and Literature* 20 (3): 236–256.

Whiteley, Sara, and David Peplow. 2020. Interpreting real and fictional worlds in interaction: A socio-cognitive approach to reading group talk. *Text and Talk* 41 (1): 119–139.

Williams, Raymond. 2010. The tenses of the imagination. In *Tenses of imagination: Raymond Williams on science fiction, utopia and dystopia*, ed. Andrew Milner, 113–124. Bern: Peter Lang.

CHAPTER 7

Conclusion

Abstract This chapter brings together the overall findings of the book and summarises its key points.

Keywords COVID-19 • Lockdown • Reading habits

1 Introduction

In this book, to our knowledge, the only applied linguistic analysis of the UK public's reading in the first lockdown of 2020, we set out to examine how participants completing our survey reflected on any changes in their reading habits. In the next section, we briefly summarise the findings of each of our chapters.

2 Summary of Findings

In Chap. 2, we looked at forms and genres of reading and examined how participants discussed their preferences for particular forms and genres of fiction. Our findings showed that participants gravitated slightly less towards genre fiction during the lockdown than they did before it. Where genre preferences were stated, readers indicated that they were drawn to

© The Author(s), under exclusive license to Springer Nature
Switzerland AG 2024
A. Boucher et al., *Reading Habits in the COVID-19 Pandemic*,
https://doi.org/10.1007/978-3-031-52753-1_7

particular genres because these provided a sense of escapism, catharsis, and an opportunity to learn and empathise with fictional characters and their situations. Intriguingly, darker genres such as gothic and post-apocalyptic fiction were given as example genres as was crime fiction, the latter providing a contrasting sense of familiarity in its plots, tropes, and characters despite its content. We also highlighted how, among those who conversely did not select these genres, avoidance was often framed within comments such as 'too close for comfort' and 'too close to home', where in these instances, the alignment of the fictional worlds with the real-life experience of living through the pandemic felt too familiar for some readers. Our data revealed different kinds of readers: those who wanted to confront demands of lockdown and pandemic by reading books that were similar and those who wanted to avoid it altogether. We revealed a complex picture in terms of how readers viewed particular genres, with readers sometimes having contradictory understandings of their own reading habits but a good sense of their emotional and cognitive needs and how these might be met by specific genres of fiction.

In Chap. 3, we examined how readers discussed time, how they felt time was gained, lost, and used during the lockdown in relation to their reading habits, and how they perceived reading itself as a phenomenon. In our free-text responses, we found that 'time' was most frequently occurring noun, and often quantified and presented metaphorically as a resource, a commodity or something of value. Nearly 60% of participants said they were spending more time reading during lockdown, but again we found a complex picture emerging. Commuting is often a time spent reading, but we found participants reported differences in the loss of a commute on their reading. Some reported that time had been gained and could now be used for reading; for others, the loss of a commute took away a dedicated space for reading that had now been filled with other demands. Similarly, time given to caring responsibilities often impacted on space for reading, whereas for others it provided an opportunity to read. As our findings in other chapters demonstrate, some participants spoke of reading supporting their mental health, whereas some reported being unable to spend time reading due to anxieties over the lockdown. We found that readers often drew on immersion and transportation metaphors to describe their ability (or not) to be moved into a fictional world. Our data also revealed that some participants framed reading as an agentive figure carrying out actions on them; one interesting pattern of representation was reading as a kind of caregiver, providing stability and therapeutic benefits.

7 CONCLUSION   127

In Chap. 4, we continued to examine the perceived therapeutic benefits of reading. We examined the top 100 keywords in our free-text sub-corpus, focusing on those that were thematically grouped as relating to specific reasons participants provided for reading during the lockdown period. We examined how 'comfort' and 'comforting' were strongly associated with other nouns denoting mental/sensory experiences such as 'familiarity', 'enjoyment', 'relaxation', 'distraction', and 'nostalgia'. Here we outlined how participants framed responses around these words within an overall sense, in a similar way to how they spoke of specific genres, of providing security. Our analysis of wordforms of 'escape' and 'escaping' highlighted an explicit example of a transportation metaphor as some of our participants outlined how they used reading as a tool to move away from the realities of the lockdown and the pandemic. As we indicated in Chaps. 2 and 3, participants' experiences of lockdown were not uniform; for example, we found that some participants sought escapism through reading, whereas others found that they were unable to transport themselves into fictional worlds because the anxiety associated with lockdown was too great. In these instances, the metaphors of transportation and immersion were not ones that participants could associate themselves with or use.

In Chap. 5, we turned to look at how participants answered questions on re-reading in relation to the lockdown. We highlighted how participants reported that they tended to re-read during the lockdown for comfort, to relive emotional responses to books, to be transported into a familiar and comforting fictional world, and to appreciate good writing. These all appeared to mitigate the effects of lockdown on mental health. As in Chaps. 3 and 4, we highlighted how participants who said that they had re-read books during the lockdown drew on particular metaphors. We examined how these included metaphors of reading as a relationship and specifically a friend, warmth metaphors where reading was described by participants as cosy and providing comfort, and reading as an emotional support that provided a sense of nostalgia and, in many cases, was explicitly described as a kind of medicine. We also expanded on some of our findings from Chap. 4 on reading and escapism, here specifically aligned with how participants reported their re-reading practices. Our participants spoke highly of re-reading (using a journey metaphor) because the ending of a re-read book was familiar and offered a secure place of refuge.

Finally, Chap. 6 examined some of the changing practices in reading that arose as a result of the lockdown. Although our participants were responding at a relatively early stage of the pandemic, we analysed some interesting trends that seemed to emerge as a result of reduced opportunities to connect with other reads in face-to-face contexts. Here, we highlighted how reading groups were already moving online to make use of the affordances of modern technology and how these practices were discussed and represented by participants with, for example, 'zoom' fulfilling a range of grammatical, lexical, and discourse functions. We also explored how participants coped more generally with lockdown constraints and how these impacted on the kinds of people with whom they now regularly discussed books. We showed that many participants were restricted to discussing books with family, but that, for some, this reopened the domestic setting as a space for discussing books. Equally, new semi-public spaces such as the 'bubble' or discussions in parks and other open spaces emerged together with online spaces as participants made use of social media as a way of connecting with other readers. Overall, we highlight that participants sought to refashion social reading in a variety of ways according to their own contexts and their own needs.

3 Conclusion

This book has provided a unique and valuable overview of the UK public's reading habits and how these changed and were influenced by the first lockdown period of 2020. Although our study was focused solely on the first lockdown, it provides an important overview and analysis of the impact of the COVID-19 pandemic on public reading habits.

We are aware, however, that there are limitations in terms of the extent to which we can form general conclusions, particularly given that aside from the participants' ages (which varied broadly), respondents generally fit a quite specific demographic. For example, just over 80% of those who completed the survey were women, corresponding with the generally accepted notion in the twenty-first century that 'books remain the province of white women' (Price 2019, p. 64; see also Davies et al. 2022, p. 19). Even aside from these demographic realities, it seems likely that only those who were already interested in reading would have taken the time to complete the survey. Equally, the participants in our survey form a self-selecting sample of people who value reading sufficiently to voluntarily engage with our research project and so it is likely that most, if not all, enjoyed reading at childhood and have continued to read into adult life.

Our study also demonstrates that there are a wide range of reasons as to why participants read, what genres they read, how much they read, what they used reading for, whether they re-read, and how they discussed reading with others and in specific social spaces. We are mindful of the importance of remembering that although the lockdown was effectively experienced by everyone in the UK, not everyone had the same lockdown experience, and people were living in situations with very different demands and constraints on their lives.[1] Undoubtedly, this can account for some of the differences that we have highlighted and discussed in each of our chapters.

As we write this conclusion, we are also aware that there is still much we can learn about how the first lockdown and subsequent ones impacted on readers and reading practices as well as on how these practices connect, for example, to wider contexts of education, health, and economic wellbeing. We hope, however, that this book provides a narrative that, in time, will form part of a wider picture that helps us to understand how COVID-19 affected—and affects—people. For as we write, the threat of COVID-19 continues to exist, with new variants both in existence and expected in the future. It remains to be seen exactly what the future impact will be on the themes and topics explored in this book.

References

Clayton, Carmen, Rafe Clayton, and Marie Potter. 2020. *British families in lockdown: Initial findings*. Leeds Trinity University/UKRI.

Davies, Ben, Christina Lupton, and Johanne Gormsen Schmidt. 2022. *Reading novels during the Covid-19 pandemic*. Oxford: Oxford University Press.

Price, Leah. 2019. *What we talk about when we talk about books*. New York: Basic Books.

---

[1] See, for example, Clayton et al. (2020) who interview 60 parents from a range of different backgrounds about the first lockdown, highlighting significant differences in experience.

Appendix 1 *The Lockdown Library Project*: Survey Questions

1. [Consent statement]
2. What is your age?
   18–30
   31–40
   41–50
   51–60
   61–70
   70+
3. What is your occupation?
4. What is your gender?
5. Since the start of the lockdown, I have been reading
   (a) About the same amount as I would normally
   (b) Less than I would normally
   (c) More than I would normally
5a. If you have answered b) or c) above, why do you think this is the case? Please give details.
6. Since the start of the lockdown, I have been reading
   (a) At about the same speed as I would normally
   (b) Slower than I would normally
   (c) Faster than I would normally

6a. If you have answered b) or c) above, why do you think this is the case? Please give details.
7. Before the lockdown, I preferred to read:
   - Physical books
   - On an e-reader (e.g. Kindle)
   - Audiobooks
   - Other
7a. If you selected 'Other', please specify.
8. Since the start of the lockdown, I have preferred to read
   - Physical books
   - On an e-reader (e.g. Kindle)
   - Audiobooks
   - Other
8a. If you selected 'Other', please specify.
8b. If you have observed differences between your answers to the last two questions, please comment on why you think this is the case.
9. Before the lockdown, did you typically discuss your reading experiences with others?
9a. If you answered 'Yes' to Q9 in what contexts did you discuss your reading experiences? Please select all that apply: [option to include an additional comment for each].
   - Face to face (in person)
   - Face to face (via video call such as Facetime or Skype)
   - Over the phone
   - Via social media (if so, which platforms)
   - Via online review sites (if so, which sites)
   - Other (please specify)
9b. Before lockdown, how frequently did you discuss your reading experiences with others?
   - More than once a week
   - About once every week
   - About once every couple of weeks
   - About once every month
   - About once every couple of months
   - Other (please specify)

APPENDIX 1 THE LOCKDOWN LIBRARY PROJECT: SURVEY QUESTIONS   133

10. Since the start of lockdown, have you discussed your reading experiences with others?
10a. If you answered 'Yes' to Q10 in what contexts have you discussed your reading experiences? Please select all that apply: [option to include an additional comment for each]
- Face to face (in person)
- Face to face (via video call such as Facetime or Skype)
- Over the phone
- Via social media (if so, which platforms)
- Via online review sites (if so, which sites)
- Other (please specify)

10b. Before lockdown, how frequently did you discuss your reading experiences with others?
- More than once a week
- About once every week
- About once every couple of weeks
- About once every month
- About once every couple of months
- Other (please specify)

11. Please indicate to what extent you agree or disagree with the following statements.

i) Before the lockdown, I was drawn to particular forms or genres.
- Strongly agree
- Agree
- Neither agree nor disagree
- Disagree
- Strongly disagree

ii) Since the start of the lockdown, I have been drawn to particular forms or genres.
- Strongly agree
- Agree
- Neither agree nor disagree
- Disagree
- Strongly disagree

iii) Since the start of the lockdown, I have been avoiding particular forms or genres.
- Strongly agree
- Agree
- Neither agree nor disagree

- Disagree
- Strongly disagree

iv) Since the start of the lockdown, I have been avoiding particular forms or genres.
- Strongly agree
- Agree
- Neither agree nor disagree
- Disagree
- Strongly disagree

12. Before the lockdown, which forms of fiction did you prefer to read? Please select all that apply.
    - Graphic novels
    - Novels
    - Plays
    - Poetry
    - Short Stories

13. Since the start of the lockdown, which forms of fiction have you preferred reading? Please select all that apply.
    - Graphic novels
    - Novels
    - Plays
    - Poetry
    - Short Stories

14. If you have been drawn to particular text forms during the lockdown period, why do you think this is the case? Please give details.

15. Before the lockdown, which genres of fiction did you prefer to read? Please select all that apply.
    - Action and adventure
    - Children's literature
    - Classic and realist literature
    - Comedy and satire
    - Detective and crime fiction
    - Fairy tales
    - Fantasy
    - Historical fiction
    - Horror and Gothic fiction
    - Myths, fables, legends
    - Post-apocalyptic fiction
    - Romance

- Science and speculative fiction
- Thriller
- Other

15a. If you selected 'Other', please specify.
16. Since the start of the lockdown, which genres of fiction have you preferred reading? Please select all that apply.
    - Action and adventure
    - Children's literature
    - Classic and realist literature
    - Comedy and satire
    - Detective and crime fiction
    - Fairy tales
    - Fantasy
    - Historical fiction
    - Horror and Gothic fiction
    - Myths, fables, legends
    - Post-apocalyptic fiction
    - Romance
    - Science and speculative fiction
    - Thriller
    - Other

16a. If you selected 'Other', please specify.
17. If you have been drawn to particular genres during the lockdown period, why do you think this is the case? Please give details.
18. Before the lockdown, which forms of fiction did you avoid reading? Please select all that apply.
    - Graphic novels
    - Novels
    - Plays
    - Poetry
    - Short Stories
19. Since the start of the lockdown, which forms of fiction have you avoided reading? Please select all that apply.
    - Graphic novels
    - Novels
    - Plays
    - Poetry
    - Short Stories

20. If you have been avoiding particular forms during the lockdown period, why do you think this is the case? Please give details.
21. Before the lockdown, which genres of fiction did you avoid reading? Please select all that apply.
    - Action and adventure
    - Children's literature
    - Classic and realist literature
    - Comedy and satire
    - Detective and crime fiction
    - Fairy tales
    - Fantasy
    - Historical fiction
    - Horror and Gothic fiction
    - Myths, fables, legends
    - Post-apocalyptic fiction
    - Romance
    - Science and speculative fiction
    - Thriller
    - Other

21a. If you selected 'Other', please specify.

22. Since the start of the lockdown, which genres of fiction have you avoided reading? Please select all that apply.
    - Action and adventure
    - Children's literature
    - Classic and realist literature
    - Comedy and satire
    - Detective and crime fiction
    - Fairy tales
    - Fantasy
    - Historical fiction
    - Horror and Gothic fiction
    - Myths, fables, legends
    - Post-apocalyptic fiction
    - Romance
    - Science and speculative fiction
    - Thriller
    - Other

22a. If you selected 'Other', please specify.

23. If you have been avoiding particular genres during the lockdown period, why do you think this is the case? Please give details.
24. Do you re-read books?
    (a) Yes, frequently
    (b) Yes, sometimes
    (c) Occasionally
    (d) Never
24a. Since the start of lockdown, I have re-read books
    (a) About the same amount as I would normally
    (b) Less than I would normally
    (c) More than I would normally
24b. Which books (e.g. specific titles) or types of books (e.g. genres) do you re-read normally?
24c. Which books (e.g. specific titles) or types of books (e.g. genres) have you been re-reading since the start of the lockdown?
24d. Before the lockdown, why do you re-read books?
24e. Since the start of the lockdown, why have you been re-reading books?
24f. Do you think your re-reading habits have changed during the lockdown?
24fi. If yes, please provide details of how your reading habits have changed.

Appendix 2 Top 10 Open Questions by Total Response Token Count

Rank	Open question topic	Open question prompt	Question response count	Token count
1	Reading Quantity	5.a. If you have answered b) or c) above, why do you think this is the case? Please give details.	668	11,567
2	Lockdown Genre Preferences	17. If you have been drawn to particular genres during the lockdown period, why do you think this is the case? Please give details.	399	9330
3	Normal Re-reading Habits	24.b. Which books (e.g. specific titles) or types of books (e.g. genres) do you re-read normally?	610	7873
4	Normal Re-reading Habits	24.d. Before the lockdown, why did you re-read books?	600	7019
5	Lockdown Genre Preferences	23. If you have been avoiding particular genres during the lockdown period, why do you think this is the case? Please give details.	323	6296
6	Lockdown Genre Preferences	14. If you have been drawn to particular text forms during the lockdown period, why do you think this is the case? Please give details.	300	6197

(*continued*)

140 APPENDIX 2 TOP 10 OPEN QUESTIONS BY TOTAL RESPONSE TOKEN COUNT

(continued)

Rank	Open question topic	Open question prompt	Question response count	Token count
7	Lockdown Re-reading Habits	24.e. Since the start of the lockdown, why have you been re-reading books?	541	5859
8	Lockdown Re-reading Habits	24.c. Which books (e.g. specific titles) or types of books (e.g. genres) have you been re-reading since the start of the lockdown?	556	5571
9	Lockdown Reading Mode	8.b. If you have observed differences between your answers to the last two questions, please comment on why you think this is the case.	215	5161
10	Lockdown Re-reading Habits	24.f.i. Please provide details of how your re-reading habits have changed	269	4713
Total			4481	69,586

Appendix 3 Top 100 Keywords in the Free-Text Portion of the *Aston Lockdown Reading Survey* Corpus

Rank	Word	Frequency		Relative Frequency (Per Million Tokens)		Keyness Score
		Lockdown Corpus	enTenTen20	Lockdown Corpus	enTenTen20	
1	Goodreads	239	36,266	2757	1	1736
2	Re-read	226	89,188	2607	1	1065
3	Reread	136	75,149	1569	1	707
4	Escapism	84	30,898	969	1	646
5	Re-reading	93	42,177	1073	1	637
6	Rereading	64	32,914	738	1	482
7	Lockdown	394	666,783	4544	11	384
8	Audiobooks	58	45,871	669	1	384
9	Post-apocalyptic	43	52,573	496	1	268
10	Whatsapp	106	229,895	1223	4	259
11	Novels	315	853,824	3633	14	245
12	Favourites	93	243,306	1073	4	217
13	Austen	42	83,459	484	1	206
14	Pratchett	23	22,001	265	0	196
15	Genres	140	454,258	1615	7	193
16	e-reader	22	20,300	254	0	192
17	Escapist	22	20,857	254	0	190
18	Fiction	452	1,831,915	5213	30	170

(*continued*)

(continued)

Rank	Word	Frequency Lockdown Corpus	Frequency enTenTen20	Relative Frequency Lockdown Corpus	Relative Frequency enTenTen20	Keyness Score
19	Classics	143	547,061	1649	9	167
20	Non-fiction	50	151,770	577	2	167
21	Thrillers	28	60,958	323	1	163
22	Commuting	43	132,299	496	2	158
23	Comforting	60	221,547	692	4	151
24	Familiarity	66	253,796	761	4	149
25	Dystopian	28	76,393	323	1	145
26	Bookclub	12	3691	138	0	132
27	Wodehouse	13	13,521	150	0	124
28	Kindle	66	325,140	761	5	121
29	Furloughed	16	34,988	185	1	118
30	Commute	46	225,201	531	4	114
31	Dreamwidth	10	3401	115	0	110
32	Tumblr	22	81,915	254	1	109
33	Agatha	19	62,948	219	1	109
34	Revisit	42	216,648	484	4	107
35	Heyer	11	12,234	127	0	107
36	Concentrate	102	619,228	1176	10	107
37	Netgalley	10	5986	115	0	106
38	Georgette	11	16,211	127	0	101
39	Eyre	16	53,175	185	1	100
40	Sayers	12	27,002	138	0	97
41	Instagram	138	953,500	1592	15	97
42	Romance	122	875,245	1407	14	93
43	Romances	17	70,002	196	1	92
44	ebooks	30	171,939	346	3	92
45	Apocalyptic	22	113,085	254	2	90
46	Books	1036	8,225,416	11,949	134	89
47	Fanfiction	12	35,420	138	1	89
48	Revisiting	19	95,665	219	2	86
49	Fb	34	221,368	392	4	86
50	Twitter	289	2,437,167	3333	40	82
51	Dickens	21	125,922	242	2	80
52	Audiobook	13	56,500	150	1	79
53	Comfort	239	2,109,978	2757	34	78
54	Pre-lockdown	7	2876	81	0	78
55	Realist	16	86,101	185	1	77
56	Enjoyment	56	460,415	646	7	76
57	Wuthering	8	14,371	92	0	76

(continued)

(continued)

Rank	Word	Frequency Lockdown Corpus	Frequency enTenTen20	Relative Frequency (Per Million Tokens) Lockdown Corpus	Relative Frequency (Per Million Tokens) enTenTen20	Keyness Score
58	Middlemarch	7	5245	81	0	75
59	Trollope	8	16,977	92	0	73
60	Reading	865	8,732,999	9977	142	70
61	Distractions	23	176,309	265	3	69
62	Poetry	168	1,713,384	1938	28	67
63	Facebook	309	3,269,574	3564	53	66
64	Detective	60	603,552	692	10	64
65	Bookshops	8	28,784	92	0	64
66	Autobiographies	7	17,750	81	0	64
67	Distracted	33	320,257	381	5	62
68	sff	7	20,478	81	0	61
69	Gatsby	9	46,007	104	1	60
70	Mantel	8	34,652	92	1	60
71	Depressing	22	203,094	254	3	59
72	Immerse	15	119,831	173	2	59
73	Potter	48	539,814	554	9	57
74	Nonfiction	16	140,590	185	2	57
75	Ereader	6	15,417	69	0	56
76	Fan-fiction	5	3714	58	0	55
77	Hardbacks	5	3853	58	0	55
78	Nostalgia	24	250,713	277	4	55
79	Popsugar	5	4512	58	0	55
80	e-books	11	82,551	127	1	55
81	Hobb	5	4832	58	0	54
82	Christie	21	218,516	242	4	54
83	Avoided	59	727,613	681	12	53
84	Discord	15	145,186	173	2	52
85	Atwood	8	52,750	92	1	50
86	Avoiding	60	789,515	692	13	50
87	Messenger	38	479,324	438	8	50
88	eg	42	537,690	484	9	50
89	Omens	6	27,533	69	0	49
90	Fantasy	112	1,591,296	1292	26	48
91	Distraction	23	281,412	265	5	48
92	Concentrating	19	222,058	219	4	48
93	Biographies	15	166,607	173	3	47
94	Socialising	6	31,464	69	1	47
95	Scifi	6	32,570	69	1	46
96	Favourite	94	1,410,740	1084	23	45

(continued)

(continued)

Rank	Word	Frequency Lockdown Corpus	Frequency enTenTen20	Relative Frequency (Per Million Tokens) Lockdown Corpus	Relative Frequency (Per Million Tokens) enTenTen20	Keyness Score
97	Graphic	83	1,246,531	957	20	45
98	Blm	12	130,447	138	2	45
99	Noughts	4	3589	46	0	45
100	Librarything	5	20,431	58	0	44

Index[1]

A
Applied linguistics, 3, 4
Audience, 14, 16–19, 22, 34
Austen, Jane, 90

B
Black Lives Matter (BLM) Movement, 33, 118
Book sales, 15

C
Caring responsibilities, 41–42, 48–49, 58
Catharsis, 18, 19, 28–29, 35
Characterisation, 92
Children's literature, 22, 27, 35
Cognitive Grammar (CG), 55, 56
Collocation, 51, 52, 68, 70n4
Comfort, 88, 89, 91–96, 99, 100
Comfort reading, 70, 73
Complicity, 31, 33–34
Conceptual metaphors
  books are friends, 92, 93, 96, 98, 100
  reading is a caregiver, 57, 58, 58n4
  reading is immersion, 49, 50
  reading is transportation, 49, 50
  re-reading is (emotional) support, 94–96
  re-reading is a journey, 91, 96–99
  re-reading is a relationship, 91–94
  re-reading is medicine, 96
  time is a commodity, 53, 54
  TIME IS A RESOURCE, 52, 54
  TIME IS MONEY, 52, 54
Conceptual Metaphor Theory, 40, 84
Construal, 40, 47, 51, 54–58, 87
Coping strategy, 63–79
Corpus-assisted discourse studies (CADS), 64, 67
Corpus linguistics, 4, 6, 7, 67
COVID-19, 129

---

[1] Note: Page numbers followed by 'n' refer to notes.

INDEX

Crime fiction, 16, 18, 22, 24, 35
　See also Detective fiction
Critical race theory, 33

D
Detective fiction, 21, 33, 35
　See also Crime fiction
Discourse analysis, 68
Distraction, 64, 70, 73–79

E
Endings, 99–100
Escape, 28, 31, 32
Escapism, 64, 65, 73–76, 78, 79, 90, 100, 126, 127

F
Fairy tales, 22, 24, 27, 35
Familiarity, 70, 73–75, 79
Fantasy fiction, 26, 35
Framing, 87, 91–93, 96

G
Genre, 67, 70, 74, 76, 125–127, 129
Genre fiction, definition of, 16–19
'Gone-Girl-on-a-Train,' 17, 18, 33
Gothic fiction, 20

H
Happily Ever After (HEA), 22, 28, 30, 35
Horror, 16, 20, 29, 35

K
Keyness analysis, 64, 67, 68, 79

L
Librarians, 110
Libraries, 2
'Literary' fiction, 16, 17, 28, 34
Literature of sensibility, 22
Lockdown, 1–5, 8, 40–47, 49–51, 53, 54, 57, 58
Lockdown restrictions, 114
　bubbles, 114–116

M
Mass reading event (MRE), 106, 107
Melodrama, 20, 22
Mental health, 19, 21, 28, 31–32, 43, 49–51, 56, 58, 126, 127
Metaphors, 126, 127

N
Natural world, 116
Nostalgia, 70, 72–74
Novel reading, 116
Novel, the rise of, 19

O
Open questions, 64, 66–68, 71, 72, 74, 75, 77, 79

P
Pandemic time, 115, 117–120
Post-apocalyptic fiction, 23, 26, 29, 30, 32
Predictability, 84, 85, 89, 90, 99–101
Proximity, 31–32

Q
Qualitative research, 6
Quantitative research, 6

INDEX

R
Reading as agent, 51, 54–58
Reading class, 116
Reading communities, 106, 116, 117
Reading culture, 110, 112, 114, 116
Reading habits, 2–5, 3n3, 7, 9
Reading practices
 domestic reading, 115
 feminist critique of, 107
 social reading, 106–121
 solitary reading, 107
Reading 2.0, 108–110
Re-reading, 67, 70, 72–74, 79, 84–101, 127
Richard and Judy's Book Club, 106, 107
Romance, 16, 22, 23, 26, 27, 30, 35
Ruritanian fiction, 22

S
Scenario, 91, 96–99
Science and speculative fiction, 23, 26
Security, 27, 29–30, 64, 69–74, 79
Sensation fiction, 20, 21, 28
Sketch Engine, 68, 70n4, 75, 77
Social isolation, 107
Social media
 Bookstagram, 109
 BookTok, 109
 BookTube, 109
 Discord, 118
 Facebook, 117–119
 Instagram, 109, 120
 POPSUGAR, 118, 118n2
 Storygraph, 118
 Twitter, 120

Social reading, 128
Space
 domestic space, 117
 semi-public space, 116
Sub-genre, 16, 23

T
Technological change, 112, 121
Television
 as a distraction, 47
 watching, 47, 48
Thematic coding, 6
Thriller, 16, 17, 23, 29, 35
Time, 126, 128, 129
 leisure time, 40, 42, 52, 53
 time working, 40, 42, 46, 48, 49
 use of time, 40, 42, 45, 46, 48, 49, 53
Transportation Theory, 66
Trauma, 14, 19–22, 58
Travel
 'commute appreciation,' 42, 45
 commuting, 45
 'travel based multi-tasking, 42

U
Utopian fiction, 22

V
Video-conferencing software
 Facetime, 113
 Microsoft Teams, 109, 112
 Skype, 112
 Zoom, 109, 112–114

Printed in the United States
by Baker & Taylor Publisher Services